PITMAN BUSINESS TYPEWRITING

Frederick Heelis

Vertical Method

Sixth edition by
Janette Malempré
Director, Pitmans College, Wimbledon

Pitman

GU00790206

PITMAN BOOKS LIMITED
128 Long Acre, London WC2E 9AN

Associated Companies
Pitman Publishing Pty Ltd, Melbourne
Pitman Publishing New Zealand Ltd, Wellington

© Pitman Publishing Ltd 1971, 1977

Sixth edition 1977
Reprinted 1978, 1980, 1982

British Library CIP Data

Heelis, Frederick
Business typewriting: Vertical method.—6th ed
1. Typewriting
I. Title II. Malempre, J
652.3'024   Z49

Text set in Monotype Baskerville,
printed by photolithography and bound in Great Britain
at The Pitman Press, Bath

ISBN 0 273 01067 0

PREFACE

In this edition, BUSINESS TYPEWRITING has been brought up to date to maintain its suitability for students preparing for typewriting examinations up to the standard required for R.S.A. Stage II, and some exercises have been introduced which are in line with current examination papers.

The margin-stop settings suggested, for both pica and elite type, are based on the use of international paper sizes A4 and A5.

The book is intended primarily for students working under the guidance of a teacher, and for this reason instructions have been kept to a minimum.

However, for the benefit of the student working on her own the following advice is given:—

1. To assist you in becoming acquainted with your typewriter, study the Instruction Manual which is provided by typewriter manufacturers. Properly maintained, regularly cleaned and used with skill, a typewriter will produce work of the highest quality and you will find that there are many mechanical aids on the typewriter to assist with the display of your work.

2. Correct posture is vital for good typewriting technique, so ensure that you always sit well to the rear of your chair in an erect position with your back supported and both feet placed firmly on the floor.

3. The edge of your typewriter should be level with the edge of your desk; your forearms should be sloping parallel to the keyboard.

4. Use a sheet of stout paper as a backing sheet in order to protect the platen of your typewriter. Insert the paper with the left edge at "O" on the front scale and make sure that the top edge of the paper is straight (this can be done by using the paper release lever).

Exercise 204

Before typing the following specification read the notes on page 80

SPECIFICATION for supplying, delivering and erecting ventilation to the Planning Office at 416 Balham High Road, Leicester.

May, 19—

SUPPLY, DELIVER AND ERECT

One air input plant capable of providing 10 air changes to the above-mentioned area. The system would consist of a centrifugal fan mounted on the roof to which we would attach a filter to the inlet and a heater battery on the discharge side.

The heater would then be connected to a system of ductwork splitting two ways and running through the two laylights existing in the low area of the office and suitable distribution ductwork running along the centre portion of the Main Office Area. This portion would be fitted with the necessary two-way directional type grilles.

To ensure a positive air movement across the office we would also provide two exhaust roof units fitted on the glazed portion of the roof nearest the corridor.

Details of the equipment are as follows:–

AIR SUPPLY PLANT

FAN

This would be of the centrifugal type capable of delivering 10,000 c.f.m. of tempered air against the resistance of the system when running at 448 r.p.m. and driven by a $5\frac{1}{2}$ h.p. weatherproof motor wound for an electrical supply of 415 volts, three phase, 50 cycles. For controlling the above we include for one hand operated starter. The above fan and motor set would be complete with the necessary drive and guard and mounted on channel iron base plate with anti-vibration mountings.

FILTER

This would be of the side withdrawal type fitted with 15 filter units mounted in specially adapted frames suitable for easy cleaning. The filter would be complete with the necessary cowling to prevent the rain coming into the air stream and the necessary change section to the inlet of the fan.

HEATER BATTERY

This would be of the gilled tube type capable of raising 10,000 c.f.m. from $-1°C$ to $20°C$ when supplied with steam at 21 N/m^2. The size of the casing would be approximately 1067 mm × 1143 mm high and fitted with one row of gilled tubes, the tubes being fitted with aluminium fins and for controlling the heater battery we would provide one Z monotronic box, thermostat and

motorised valve complete with the necessary change section to connect on to the discharge side of the fan.

DUCTWORK

The discharge side of the heater battery would be split two ways equally into two sections, each section routing its way through each of the two laylights adjacent to the fan area. The ductwork would then be routed around the side walls of the office finishing in two header ducts, each approximately 10 m long. Each header duct would have six two-way directional type grilles fitted. All external ductwork from the discharge of the heater to the laylights would be lagged with 25 mm thick polystyrene. The ductwork would be fabricated in heavy gauge galvanised sheet steel suitably stiffened and adequately supported.

EXHAUST ROOF UNIT

Each of the two units would be capable of exhausting 5,000 c.f.m. against free air conditions and would be fitted with louvred shutters. Each fan unit would be running at 700 r.p.m. and would absorb 0·8 amps and would be suitable for an electrical supply of 415 volts, three phase 50 cycles. The casings would be suitable for fitting to your glazed section of the roof. For controlling the above units we would provide two Square 'D' direct-on-line push button starters.

ERECTION

We include for the services of all necessary skilled and unskilled labour for erecting this equipment on prepared foundations at site during our normal working hours. Should our materials arrive on site in advance of our erectors we have assumed that you will arrange for the necessary unloading and suitable storage free of charge.

PRICE

£1,800 (One thousand eight hundred pounds). This price is nett and includes for delivery to site and erection as stated above.

DELIVERY

Delivery could be effected in 8/10 weeks.

PACKING

Packing would be charged at cost and credited in full if returned to us carriage paid in good condition within six weeks.

GENERAL

We refer to our attached Standard Conditions of Trading.

CONTENTS

Exercise 203

Type the basic menu sheet omitting the handwritten details. Take two carbon copies. Re-insert the top copy into your typewriter and type in the menus for the week beginning 8th March.

   As additional exercises compose menus for the weeks beginning 15th and 22nd March and type in the details on the carbon copies.

SCHOOL   MEALS   SERVICE

CENTRAL   KITCHEN, Chalford Road.

Menu for the week beginning   *8th March*

Monday	Sausages Mashed Potatoes Peas	Apple pie & Custard
Tuesday	Meat Pie Creamed Pots. Cabbage	Lemon Sponge Pudding
Wednesday	Roast Beef Roast Pots. Carrots	Fruit Salad & Custard
Thursday	Cornish Pasty Creamed Pots. Peas	Ginger Pudding & Golden Syrup
Friday	Cheese and Egg Flan Mashed Pots. Beans in Tomato Sauce	Rice Pudding

INDEX

Exercise 202

Type this letter for dispatch to the following people:-

W. KEARSLEY ESQ., B.A.,
Head of Sports Department,
Central Comprehensive School,
Bingley, Yorkshire
BJ 16 2AY

R. J. MURPHY ESQ.,
Headmaster, M.A.,
Upton Grammar
School,
Upton, Somerset
UP 29 6ZQ

Miss B. M. ACTON M.A.,
Headmistress,
Pankhurst Girls' School,
Radlett, Herts
RJ 72 5BD

Dear Sir/Madam,
    You will, no doubt, be giving consideration to the question of sports equipment for the coming winter season, and we trust you will find the catalogue, which we are sending you under separate cover, of assistance. The prices quoted allow us the lowest workable margin of profit, but on regular orders we shall be glad to allow you a discount of five per cent from the list prices.
    You may possibly be quoted larger discounts by competing firms, but we think you will realize that in such cases an additional profit is added to the price in order to provide a margin for extra discount.
    We invite you to call here to inspect our stock. However, if this is inconvenient we shall be happy to submit samples of any articles you require.
Yours faithfully,

ELEMENTARY KEYBOARD WORK

The Home Keys

The four letters **a s d** and **f** are the **home keys for the left hand.** Place the little finger of the left hand on **a,** the guide key for the left hand, and the other fingers in order over **s d** and **f.** Here the fingers should rest when not being used for other keys.

It is important that you should learn to place your fingers on the home keys without looking at the keyboard. Practise doing this.

Treat the **right hand** in the same way, placing the little finger on **;,** the guide key for the right hand, and the others in order over **l k** and **j.** There is an extra letter for the first finger of each hand—**g** and **h.**

When typing, keep your eyes on the exercise you are copying, and do not look at the keyboard. Listen for the bell, which rings some spaces before the end of the line, and return the carriage without taking your eyes off the copy. Keep the right hand in position on the home keys, raise the left hand and strike the carriage-return lever with the first finger of the left hand, supported by the other fingers. Keep the left hand flat, palm down, and sweep the carriage smartly back. Immediately return the left hand to the home keys.

If you are using an electric typewriter your fingers should hover *over* their home keys without actually resting on them.

Exercise 1

Margin stops: Pica 25 and 60; Elite 35 and 70

Type each line of this exercise, leaving a double-line space between each line. Do not look at your work at all until you have typed it; then you can check your work, marking each error with a pencil.

```
fgfdsa fgfdsa fgfdsa fgfdsa fgfd

jhjkl; jhjkl; jhjkl; jhjkl; jhjk

fgfdsa jhjkl; fgfdsa jhjkl; fgfd

jhjkl; fgfdsa jhjkl; fgfdsa jhjk

asdfgf ;lkjhj asdfgf ;lkjhj asdf
```

V R M and U

The following exercise introduces the first-finger letters **v** and **r** (left hand) and **m** and **u** (right hand). Keep your fingers over the home keys. Move the correct finger to the position required for striking the new key, and strike it sharply with a staccato touch: then immediately return the finger to its position over its home key.

Exercise 2

Margin stops: Pica 20 and 70; Elite 25 and 75

```
fr fr fr fr fr fr fr fr ju ju ju ju ju ju ju ju

fv fv fv fv fv fv fv fv jm jm jm jm jm jm jm jm

frfvf frfvf frfvf frfvf frfvf frfvf frfvf frfvf

jujmj jujmj jujmj jujmj jujmj jujmj jujmj jujmj

fvfrf jmjuj fvfrf jmjuj fvfrf jmjuj fvfrf jmjuj
```

I

Type the following scores on A5 paper. Centre vertically and horizontally and strike the full stops lightly.

James b Lonsdale 2
Couper c-b Lonsdale . . . 15
J. D. Stevens not out . . . 79
Thomas, C. P., lbw Jackson ... 6
Clarkson c Lonsdale b Jackson 8
Mainwaring b Lonsdale . . . 12
Thomas, J. D., c-b Lonsdale . . . 7
Hapgood c Smith b Rupert . . 56
Alexander b Lonsdale 3
Johnson run out 7
Allan st Smith b Lonsdale . . 15

Total 130
      210

Fall of wickets.— 4—23—30— 42—57—
64— 130—136— 156

Bowling — Lonsdale 12-4-57-6;
Jackson 11-2-98-2; Rupert
9-1-42-1; Ames 1-0-13-0.

B T N and Y

In the following exercise the letters **b** and **t** (left hand) and **n** and **y** (right hand) are included.

Locate these keys and strike them in the same way as the ones in the preceding exercise.

Exercise 3

Margin stops: Pica 20 and 70; Elite 25 and 75

```
fg  ft  fg  ft  fg  ft  fg  ft  jh  jy  jh  jy  jh  jy  jh  jy

fg  fb  fg  fb  fg  fb  fg  fb  jh  jn  jh  jn  jh  jn  jh  jn

fuf fur fuv fum fun fut jur juv juf jum jun jut

fyf fyr fyv fym fyn fyt jyf jyr jyt jym jyn jyb

bur bub hun hug tug tut tub nun urn fug mum tun
```

Exercise 4

Margin stops: Pica 10 and 75; Elite 20 and 85

```
fun rum gym buy guv ruv bun muv byg gun mug tub but hun rub gum

jug fur gub jur hub nuf hyb fub huv guy yun rut gur hut rug nut

hurt rung jury turn hunt ruby numb butt fury muff bury hung run

tuff runt tunt ruth fumy guff bunt mung huff mutt bung burr gut

funny hubby mummy burgh hurry furry rummy nutty muggy tuft burn

rugby runny tubby tunny turfy gummy bunny gutty burnt ruff burt
```

C E I and the COMMA

In the following exercise, the second-finger keys **c** and **e** (left hand) and **,** and **i** (right hand) are included.

Exercise 5

Margin stops: Pica 10 and 75; Elite 20 and 85

```
ded dcd ded dcd ded dcd ded dcd kik k,k kik k,k kik k,k kik k,k

ded kik dcd kik ded kik dcd k,k ded kik dcd k,k ded kik dcd k,k

did ice kid cid die dik ide eke did ice kid cid die dik ide eke
```

Type the following memos, taking two carbon copies.

MEMORANDUM

From: A Marshall, Operations Manager   Date: 21st Jan 19--

To: All Managers

Subject: <u>Telephones</u>

Please return as soon as possible the following details regarding
telephones and their situation in your hotel:

1.   The number of incoming lines and their location

2.   The number of extensions and their location

This is to include business lines, lines for your flat and any lines
going to staff accommodation.

MEMORANDUM

From: G O'Dell, Catering Controller   Date: 28th January --

To: All Managers

Subject: Hygiene Regulations

As you are no doubt aware, the Hygiene Inspections are becoming more
and more stringent and recently a well-known restaurant in Surrey
has been heavily fined for non-compliance with hygiene regulations.

Unfortunately, in a number of restaurants, insufficient attention
is given to the basic requirements regarding kitchen cleanliness
and food storage. It is imperative that all managers take a
personal interest in this side of the operation to ensure that the
necessary standards are reached and maintained.

Exercise 6

Margin stops: Pica 20 and 70; Elite 25 and 75

ethic edged edict edify educe educt egret eider

eight eking embed ember emend emery endue enemy

enter entry enure icing imbed imbue infer inker

inner inter inure itchy ivied udder umber unbid

uncut under undid undue unfit unify unite utter

Exercise 7

Margin stops: Pica 20 and 70; Elite 25 and 75

bribe brick bride bring brink birch birth biter

crier crime cider civic drift drink drive dirty

frier fifty fight fiver grief grime giddy girth

hinge hired hirer hitch miner minim mirth might

night ninth nitre rider ridge right rigid river

tribe trice trick tried trier trite trunk truth

Exercise 8

Margin stops: Pica 20 and 70; Elite 25 and 75

the chief might check the device by the evening

meet them by buying the engine the firm decided

he tried the third time but it undid the effect

the determined fire by the men defied the enemy

X W and the FULL STOP and O

In the following exercises the third-finger keys **x** and **w** (left hand) and the full stop and **o** (right hand) are introduced.

Exercise 9

Margin stops: Pica 20 and 70; Elite 25 and 75

sw xs lo .l sw xs lo .l sw xs lo .l sw xs lo .l

ws wx ol o. ws wx ol o. ws wx ol o. ws wx ol o.

sx ws l. ol sx ws l. ol sx ws l. ol sx ws l. ol

3

Display the following advertisement on A4 paper

FOR SALE

Standing Timber

Rightly described as the most important sale
of the decade.
The Rookwood Estate
Essex

64,348 cubic metres of the finest Beech in   l.c.
the land, having quarter girth of 61.0 cm & a
length without blemish up to 21.3 m.

Also a quantity of coppice (oak & ash) standing, to.
easy removal & close to railway station and
canal wharf.

To be sold in 12 lots by auction
at the Moot Hall, Rookwood
on
Friday 10th April
at 1430 hrs precisely

Illustrated catalogues (price 10p) may be
u.c.   obtained from the auctioneers:-
Messrs. Stuart, Bett, & Mills,
9 Station Road, Rookwood.

Exercise 10

Margin stops: Pica 20 and 70; Elite 25 and 75

```
wed web wey who why wig win wit woe won woo wry

see seg set shy sib sic sin sir sit ski sky sly

sob sog son sot sow soy sty sub sue sum sun sud

box fix fox mix six sox odd ode oer off oft ohm

oil oke old one orc orb ore our out owe owl own

lee led leg let lid lie lin lit log lob lot low
```

Exercise 11

Margin stops: Pica 10 and 75; Elite 20 and 85

```
follows stocked hurtful softens follows stocked hurtful softens

workers lowered outsell grounds workers lowered outsell grounds

strokes boyhood wishful lodgers strokes boyhood wishful lodgers
```

Exercise 12

Margin stops: Pica 10 and 75; Elite 20 and 85

```
they will tell you the true story of the journey over the hills

if you desire it he will send them the list of our first offers

we should like you to know they were not content with the goods

they will need fully eight weeks to get this jewellery together

they hold huge stocks of dried fruit in our two new town stores

we tried to inform them directly we received their lowest terms

the business girl should ensure the correct finish to this work

students should know the common words without seeking reference
```

Exercise 198

Type a letter to Mr. S. T. Donavan of 66 Nuneaton Court, Park Lane, Farnham, Surrey (our ref: PaB/EW/4670). Thank him for his enquiry and send a list of properties available abroad.
Don't forget to tell him we arrange special flights for prospective purchasers to inspect the properties, should he be interested. Look forward to hearing from him etc. etc. The complimentary closure is — Yours faithfully SUNHOMES LTD. Sales Manager.

Type this list of properties available abroad grouping them in countries in alphabetical order.

WHY NOT A HOME IN THE SUN? ⟶ *Centre*

Hammamet, Tunisia. Attractive modern flat (2 rooms plus kitchen and bathroom) in exclusive 2-storey block for sale fully furnished. £3,500.

St. Julians, Malta. Delightful bungalow near pleasant beach. Two bedrooms, bathroom, separate W.C., kitchen, small garden. £6,500.

Spain, (Benidorm.) Luxury flat in 4-storey modern block. 3 bedrooms, two bathrooms, large kitchen. Swimming pool, restaurant, 24-hour porter service. £8,500.

Algarve, Portugal. Beach development. Flats, bungalows and houses. Prices from £5,000.

Torremolinos, Spain. Modern flat (2 rooms) with kitchen and bathroom in large complex with swimming pool. £4,000, furniture at valuation.

Rimini, Italy. Delightful detached house. Four bedrooms and 2 bathrooms. Roof garden, swimming pool. £22,500.

Djerba, Tunisia. New development to include studio flats from £5,250, three-bedroomed terrace houses with sitting room on the upper floor from £8,500 and three and four-bedroomed detached single-storey villas from £14,500.

Portugal, (Algarve). Modernised farmhouse facing beautiful bay. Five bedrooms, 3 bathrooms, two reception rooms and various ancillary rooms. Swimming pool & walled garden. £21,500.

TYPIST. type
Please leave all numbers as figures (not words).
The list of properties is to be typed on a separate sheet for enclosure with the letter.

Words underlined to be typed in caps.

ANCILLARY

101

do the work well in order to secure the good thought of friends

now is the time for you to try to succeed in the difficult test

send them your difficulties sometimes, for they might know them

she should get the money from them in time to send in the entry

seven of the men were sent to the works to meet the instructors

tell them to try to do their best when they sit for their tests

give the girls two of the books which include full instructions

there is no doubt the men were there in time to fill the orders

Z Q $\frac{1}{2}$ and P

The following exercises include the fourth-finger keys **z** and **q** (left hand) and $\frac{1}{2}$ and **p** (right hand).

Be careful to strike the punctuation marks very lightly, so that they do not pierce the paper.

aqaza ;p;$\frac{1}{2}$; aqaza ;p;$\frac{1}{2}$; aqaza ;p;$\frac{1}{2}$; aqaza ;p;$\frac{1}{2}$; aqaza ;p;$\frac{1}{2}$; aqa

aq az ;p ;$\frac{1}{2}$ aq az ;p ;$\frac{1}{2}$ aq az ;p ;$\frac{1}{2}$ aq az ;p ;$\frac{1}{2}$ aq az ;p ;$\frac{1}{2}$ aza

aqza azqa ;p$\frac{1}{2}$; ;$\frac{1}{2}$p; aqza azqa ;p$\frac{1}{2}$; ;$\frac{1}{2}$p; aqza azqa ;p$\frac{1}{2}$; ;$\frac{1}{2}$p; ;p;

zqza qzqa $\frac{1}{2}$p$\frac{1}{2}$; p$\frac{1}{2}$p; zqza qzqa $\frac{1}{2}$p$\frac{1}{2}$; p$\frac{1}{2}$p; zqza qzqa $\frac{1}{2}$p$\frac{1}{2}$; p$\frac{1}{2}$p; ;$\frac{1}{2}$;

amazed; peoples; quiz; amazed; peoples; quiz; amazed; people; $\frac{1}{2}$

buzzing shipped 1$\frac{1}{2}$ buzzing shipped 1$\frac{1}{2}$ buzzing shipped buzzing $\frac{1}{2}$

piazza; quips; prank; quixotic; piazza; quips; prank; piazza; $\frac{1}{2}$

six ways out of the queer maze; six ways out of the queer maze;

Display the following extract from a magazine article. Use A4 paper and double-line spacing. Set margins of 2 in (51 mm) on the left and 1 in (25 mm) on the right. Centre the title AUTO-MATION. Take several carbon copies and remember that these must be free from smudges. In typewriting, italicized words are underscored.

Exercise 194

Automation represents so sharp a turning from our past ways, so abrupt a break in our old courses of action, that even many of those closely involved are not aware of the overwhelming power and scope of its revolution. Too many are still asking themselves *whether* they should automate rather than *when* and *how* they should automate. And an even greater number have failed to comprehend the nature and extent of its sociological effects.

One of the significant factors stimulating the accelerated growth of automation in both the United Kingdom and the United States has been the broad shift to automation on the continent of Europe. In Western Europe a whole new industrial structure—modern plants with automated equipment—has risen from the rubble of war. The moral is simple—to survive today, an industrial country must automate.

But (even as the representative of a company which makes machines for automation) I am concerned here about what might be called automation's human aspects—its impact upon the lives of individuals. These aspects promise to be more of a problem in the long run than the technical aspects. For while, from a technical point of view, automation is working, the same cannot be said so confidently from the human point of view. This is the area in which we must begin with increased determination to seek and find solutions—or perhaps risk social catastrophe.

A recent public opinion survey in America found that, second to Russia, unemployment caused by automation is the thing most people are worried about, and at the crux of their fears is a common failure to judge and understand the nature and extent of this development.

Change can be measured in "orders of magnitude," meaning a factor of ten-times-as-much. The computer—which with automatic machinery makes up an automated system—is some six orders of magnitude faster in its process than man—or a million-fold faster. At the same time computers can cut costs of operations by three orders of magnitude, or by something more than one thousand times.

Reproduced by kind permission of the *Sunday Times* and Mr. John Billew.

Exercise 195

On a sheet of A5 paper, display the following information:—

Invest with the CITY OF NORTHINGHAM

Mortgage Loans for 2–5 years
$9\frac{1}{2}$% for £5,000 or more
$9\frac{1}{4}$% for lesser sums
Minimum Loan £500
No expenses

For further particulars apply to:—
City Treasurer, Exchange Buildings, Northingham NN2 6QL

Exercise 196

Write a letter from your home address to the Manager of one of the banks in your town. This letter is in reply to an advertisement which appeared in the columns of your local newspaper for a shorthand-typist. Include the following information:—

You have been working for a firm of accountants, Messrs. Jackson & Phelps, since leaving school two years ago. You are employed largely on figure work at present, but having learnt shorthand-typing at evening classes, you would like to make use of this skill. Your present speeds are approximately 50 words a minute in typing and 120 words a minute in shorthand. You intend sitting for Stage III typewriting and 120 w.p.m. shorthand examinations of the R.S.A. at Whitsun. You are eighteen years of age and were educated at the local grammar school. You passed G.C.E. at Ordinary level in English language, mathematics, history, general science and art.

Give the names and addresses of three persons to whom reference may be made.

Type this exercise which uses figures and upper case characters on A5 paper.

Exercise 197

MEMORANDUM

From: J Goodwin   Date: 26th January 19– –

To: Mr D V Campbell, The Park Lane Restaurant

Subject: Car Parking

With immediate effect, would you please arrange for your car park to be closed, by means of chains, each night and opened at 10 am each morning.

You will obviously permit access to suppliers before 10 am.

Exercise 15

Margin stops: Pica 20 and 70; Elite 25 and 75

```
paced paddy padre pagan paint pairs pales palmy

paned panel panic papal paper parch parse parts

party paste pasty patch pater pause payee payer

quack quake quart queen queer quell query quest

queue quick quiet quire quite quits quota quote

dozen hazel sized wizen froze glaze prize seize
```

The Shift Keys

In the next exercise capital letters or, as they are sometimes called in typewriting, upper-case characters are included. If you examine a type bar you will find that on it there are two characters. When the shift key is in its normal position and a key is struck it is a lower-case letter or sign that will be typed. In order to bring into use the upper-case characters it is necessary to change the position of the cylinder or of the type bars, and this is done by depressing the shift key. There are two shift keys, one for each hand. When typing a capital letter on the right-hand side of the keyboard use the left-hand shift key, and vice versa. Hold the shift key down firmly with the little finger and at the same time strike the required letter.

Exercise 16

Margin stops: Pica 10 and 75; Elite 20 and 85

```
Raised Capitals are caused by releasing the Shift Key too soon.

Hold Shift Key down firmly until capital letter has been typed.

Three typewriters forwarded to your address yesterday are lost.

They asked us to telegraph to their house if we had the letter.

We shall write to the agent to say we require a freehold house.

He posted the letter to the old address, which was quite right.

She likes the fabric for the dresses, and would like hers dyed.
```

Exercise 193

The recipes set out below are wanted in booklet form. Type them in alphabetical order on two pieces of A4 paper turned sideways which are to be stapled through the centre when making up the booklet. One recipe to be typed per page. Arrange the work as attractively as possible designing a front cover for the booklet.

Marigold Wine

2 litres marigold flowers (no green stalk)
2 oranges
1 lemon
$1\frac{1}{2}$ kg sugar
4 litres water
20 gm baker's yeast

Method. Dissolve the sugar in the water and bring to the boil. Put the flowers, the thinly-peeled rind of one orange, the lemon and the fruit juice into a large bowl. Pour the hot syrup over this. Allow to cool, then add the yeast. Stir well, and leave in a warm place to ferment for a week. Strain into fermentation-jar, cover, or insert an airlock, and leave still in a warm place to ferment to a finish. Remove to a cool place and leave for three weeks before bottling.

Burnet Wine

2 litres burnet flowers
4 litres boiling water
$1\frac{1}{2}$ kg sugar
20 gm baker's yeast

Method. Put flowers and sugar into a bowl, and cover with the boiling water. Stir well. When lukewarm add the yeast mixed with a little of the liquid. Cover well, and let it stand in a warm place to ferment for fourteen days. Strain at the end of this time into a large storage bottle or jar. Cover, or insert an airlock. Let it ferment to a finish. Pour or syphon off, then bottle.

Hawthorn Berry Wine

$1\frac{3}{4}$ kg berries
4 oranges
2 lemons
9 litres boiling water
3 kg sugar, brown or white
28 gm yeast

Method. Put the berries in a large bowl, and pour the water over them. Let this stand for a week, covered, and stir daily. Strain off on to the thinly-peeled rinds and juice of the fruit. Add the sugar and stir. Warm to lukewarm and add the yeast mixed with a little of the warm liquid. Cover and leave for twenty-four hours in the large bowl. Transfer to fermentation-jar, insert an airlock, or cover well, and leave to ferment to a finish. Bottle.

These and other recipes for home-made wines may be found in "Home Made Country Wines," in the Countrywise Books series, edited by Barbara Hargreaves and published by The Farmers Weekly.

Parsley Wine

$\frac{1}{2}$ kg parsley
$1\frac{3}{4}$ kg sugar, brown or white
2 oranges
2 lemons
4 litres water
14 gm bruised root ginger, if liked
20 gm baker's yeast

Method. Boil the parsley, bruised ginger, and thinly-peeled rinds of the lemons and oranges for twenty minutes in the gallon of water. Strain on to the sugar and stir well. When lukewarm add the yeast and the fruit juice. Stir and cover. Leave for twenty-four hours. Pour into a fermentation-jar, insert an airlock, or cover with three layers of cotton material. Leave in a warm place to ferment to a finish. Syphon off into a storage jar, or bottles, and then cork.

Lemon Wine

8–10 lemons, according to size
4 litres water
$1\frac{1}{2}$ kg sugar ($1\frac{1}{2}$ kg honey can be substituted)
20 gm baker's yeast

Method. Put the thinly-peeled rind of half the lemons into a pan and bring to the boil with the water. Simmer for fifteen minutes. Put the lemon juice and the sugar into a large bowl, and pour the hot liquid over it. Stir well. When lukewarm add the yeast, mixed with a little of the warm liquid. (Some people also add some raisins.) Cover and leave for twenty-four hours in a warm place. Pour into a fermentation-jar and insert an airlock. Leave to ferment to a finish, then bottle.

Cherry Wine

$1\frac{3}{4}$ kg sweet cherries
1 kg sour cherries
4 litres water
$1\frac{3}{4}$ kg sugar
20 gm baker's yeast, or a wine yeast

Method. Chop up the fruit, put it in a large bowl, and cover with the water. Leave for three days, stirring daily. Strain through butter muslin (two layers) on to the sugar and warm to luke-warm, stirring well to dissolve the sugar. When lukewarm remove from heat, and pour into a fermentation-jar, add the yeast, cover well, or insert an airlock, and leave in a warm place to ferment. After three weeks, taste. If not sweet enough add some sugar and stir well. Leave one week or more, then bottle.

Exercise 17

Margin stops: Pica 20 and 70; Elite 25 and 75

They were ardent followers of the Constitution.

He was exasperated at the quality of the cocoa.

The etiquette of the Court surprised the youth.

This doorbell has a most annoying type of buzz.

That lazy typist does not clean her typewriter.

One of the queries should go before Parliament.

Excessive toil may not pay but laziness is bad.

Carbon copies are quite spoilt by a thumb mark.

Exercise 18

Margin stops: Pica 10 and 75; Elite 20 and 85

Three lazy labourers were exhausted by the zealous farm bailiff.

The taxicabs of France are driven at an excessive rate in Paris.

The minimum temperature in some places is the maximum in others.

An extraordinarily exciting exhibition exhausted the excise man.

Bountiful benefactors bestow beautiful abundance of benevolence.

Zealous Anzacs puzzled the lazy zebra, gazing at him in the Zoo.

Queenie is quick to question the quality of the quarterly quota.

Muffled murmurs made many remember those magnificent multitudes.

Exercise 19

Margin stops: Pica 15 and 75; Elite 25 and 85

Type the following lines. Return the carriage smartly at the end of each line. Remember to type with an even touch.

Some men learn the value of money by not having any.

A fool will be a fool whether he goes to school or not.

A man must get down to his work to get up in the world.

To do our duty and make the best of life should be our aim.

There may be noise about us but it is in silence we grow.

What man has done man can do and what has never been may be.

Exercise 192

Type the following letter to Miss S. Slimville. One carbon copy is required.

97 Farndale Way
Greenham, Middx.
Today's date

Miss S. Slimville
55 Dunster Crescent
Richmond, Surrey

Dear Sally

s.ket   I was talking to your ~~brother~~ the other day, she ~~informed~~ told me   l.c.
u.c. that you will soon be completing the secretarial course you have taken since coming down from University. She said you were anxious to obtain an appointment which would be interesting & provide opportunities for promotion & I wonder whether you would like further particulars Of the following vacancies?

To be typed
in set 4 in
single line
spacing

1. Managing Director's Secretary. Requirements:
   a. Age between 23 and 33 with even temperament.
   b. Fast shorthand/typing speeds.
   c. Ability to gain quickly a broad understanding
      of the Company's marketing, technical and
      financial organization.
   d. Hours unrestricted by personal or family obligations.
   e. Commencing salary £2,500 p.a. and car is also
      provided for personal and business use.
2. Secretary to Personnel Director.
   A first-class, practical secretary to deal with
   confidential correspondence is required for this
   responsible position in the international field.
   Besides tact and diplomacy she will need initiative,
   common sense and a desire to qualify in personnel
   administration. Salary in the range of £1,500–£2,500
   p.a. First-class education, degree essential.

I look forward to hearing from you & feel sure you will be able to obtain a position which will give you the opportunity to use your first-class training
Yours sincerely

98

Punctuation Marks—I

In the following exercises, some new punctuation marks are included. The colon is an upper-case character, on the same key as the semicolon. Notice the position of the question mark on your machine. The position of this character varies with different makes of machine. Leave two spaces after a full stop, question mark, or exclamation mark at the end of a sentence, and one space after a colon, semicolon, or comma. Some employers prefer two spaces to be left after the colon and the semicolon, and three spaces after a full stop. Remember to strike the keys for punctuation marks lightly.

Exercise 20

Margin stops: Pica 10 and 70; Elite 20 and 80

To be great and good, one must know how and when to give.

You must send him two or three every morning this year.

I am very glad he has a letter to give to each of them now.

I have had one day there but you have not been there at all.

If three of them were sent to him first, he could do it.

Is there any hope that the two men will get there in time?

Then do you not know that this thing is only for your good?

May I ask you to go out and about with him the next time?

Exercise 21

Margin stops: Pica 10 and 70; Elite 20 and 80

It is true that no man can ask more than he gives, and one who cannot take orders is not to be trusted to give them.

There are five departments in this College: Building, Business Studies, Engineering, General Studies, and Science.

I agree with you that debt is just like any other kind of trap: it is easy to get into, but hard to get out of.

Exercise 188

Set out the information given below as an advertisement for insertion in a newspaper.

CUPRESSUS LAWSONIANA. Rapid-growing evergreen hedge shrub of attractive appearance. Dark green foliage. Stands clipping well. Strong 2-yr. plants, 25 for 65p, 50 for £1·25, 100 for £2·40. Selected transplanted plants, 30–45 cm high, 88p per doz., £6·25 per 100.
BERBERIS DARUINII. Makes a lovely evergreen flowering hedge. Orange flowers in spring and summer. Plant 46 cm apart. Transplanted 2-yr. old plants, 88p per doz., £6·25 per 100.
SILVER BIRCH. Strong transplanted trees, 90–122 cm high, £1·80 per doz., £13·25 per 100. All carriage paid. RENWOOD NURSERIES, Bramley Lane, Bracknell, Berks. RG12 3RG.

Exercise 189

Display the following Menu Cover attractively on A5 paper. Note that the ornament at the end of typed or printed matter is referred to as a tailpiece.

QUEEN ANNE COLLEGE
THIRTY-THIRD
ANNUAL COMMEMORATION DINNER

Wednesday, 29th April, 19—
Sir George Lenall, C.B.E.
Chairman of the Council
presiding

—oOo—

Take at least two carbon copies of each of the following exercises, inserting the date of typing where this is not given.

Margin stops: Pica 15 and 70; Elite 24 and 79

Line-space lever for single-line spacing.

Exercise 190

4th June, 19—

The Manager,
Messrs. McAllister & Co.,
40 Frith Street, London E1 5DS
Dear Sir,

Take advantage of this special "Perfection" offer.

Because of the increased costs of raw materials, prices of desks have had to be increased. The new prices became effective on 1st June—just a few days after we had sent you our latest "Perfection" pamphlet.

Naturally we regret the necessity for the increased prices, and, because of the short space of time that elapsed between the issue of the pamphlet and the increase in price, we offer to hold open to you until 1st July the old prices (printed in black on the enclosed leaflet).

It may be a long while before you are able to buy really good desks like "Perfection" at such low prices.

Call in at our Houndsditch Showrooms and see for yourself our fine display of beautiful but inexpensive office furniture. But don't delay—the end of this month will soon be here, when the prices must go up.

Yours faithfully,
PERFECTION DESK CO. LTD.

Exercise 191

6th September, 19—

The Manager,
The Rupert Hotels Ltd.,
BOURNEMOUTH, Hants. BH5 3JH
Dear Sir,

We wish to draw your attention to a Bread-and-butter Machine we have recently put on the market.

This machine will cut slices of bread from 3 mm to 12 mm thick, and will spread the butter in the same operation, an adjustment being provided to regulate the amount of butter used.

The butter is not prepared before being put into the machine, but a water jacket is provided for use in cold weather to enable you to bring the butter to the right temperature. The butter can be put in while the machine is running, the only stoppage of the machine being for the insertion of a new loaf, which takes no more than a few seconds.

We feel sure you will realize at once the advantages of this machine, and we shall be pleased to send you a quotation upon hearing from you, or to give you a demonstration at any time you may appoint.

Yours faithfully,

Margin stops: Pica 10 and 70; Elite 20 and 80

No man is bound to be rich or great, or even wise; but every

true and worthy man is bound to be honest.

The world is moving so rapidly today that you have to run as

fast as you can to stay where you are.

The greatest pleasure is to do a good action by stealth, and

to have it found out by accident.

The Shift Lock

When it is necessary to type a number of upper-case characters in succession, **the shift lock** is brought into operation. When this key is depressed the mechanism is locked in such a position that only upper-case characters can be typed. The shift lock is released by depressing the ordinary shift key. The following exercise provides practice in the use of the shift lock.

Exercise 23

Margin stops: Pica 10 and 70; Elite 20 and 80

MARTIN CHUZZLEWIT holding LITTLE DORRIT by the hand met

BARNABY RUDGE, who said he had seen, from the window of

the OLD CURIOSITY SHOP, DOMBEY AND SON enter BLEAK HOUSE.

Thither they repaired, and when they entered found DAVID

COPPERFIELD amusing OLIVER TWIST with SKETCHES BY BOZ and

items from the PICKWICK PAPERS, and amid GREAT EXPECTATIONS,

OUR MUTUAL FRIEND, THE UNCOMMERCIAL TRAVELLER, entertaining

EDWIN DROOD with A CHRISTMAS CAROL and likewise telling him

A TALE OF TWO CITIES in HARD TIMES.

FORM LETTERS

In business, printed or duplicated letters and forms are often used on which details have to be filled in by the typist.

Make sure that the alignment scale on the front of the typewriter is carefully adjusted to the lines on the form letter. Adjust the margins and type just above the ruled lines, using the variable line-spacer if necessary.

Exercise 187

Type the following form on A5 paper with two carbon copies.

THE INSTITUTE OF OPERATIONAL RESEARCH
10 Bedford Square
London WC1B 3DP

Institute Dinner 19..
(Please use block letters or typewriter)

NAME OF COMPANY ....

NAME OF APPLICANT .... Tel. No. ....

ADDRESS FOR COMMUNICATIONS ....

....

....

NAME(S) OF GUEST(S) ....

....

REMITTANCE FOR £ .... ENCLOSED (£4·50 each)

Take the paper out of the machine. Reinsert one copy at a time in your typewriter, and fill in the details given below.

1. Company: Harrow & Wills Ltd.
   Applicant: L. Fox
   Tel. No.: 01–834 3596
   Address: 14 Wellington Road, London, WC2R 2AU
   Guests: Mrs. Mary Fox, Miss P. Fox, Mr. G. Fox
2. Company: Oulds Paper Co. Ltd.
   Applicant: A. Brownson
   Tel. No.: 01–226 4271
   Address: St. Andrews Avenue, Manchester M20 9JR
   Guests: Mr. F. Short, Mr. S. Marshall
3. Company: Grier Synthetic Fibres
   Applicant: B. Aird
   Tel. No.: 01–636 7100
   Address: 6 Bentick Street, London, W1A 1AB
   Guest: Miss G. Swanson

The Fourth Row of Keys

In the following exercises, the keys on the fourth row are included. Make sure that your finger is right over the required key, strike the key sharply and then return your finger to its home key. For signs that are the upper-case characters in the fourth row of keys, depress the shift key exactly as you do when typing capital letters and release it smartly after the key has been struck.

Some machines are not fitted with special characters for the figure one and for nought. In this case, a small "el" is used for the arabic number one and a capital "O" for a nought.

Exercise 24

Margin stops: Pica 10 and 75; Elite 20 and 85

```
w2s  o9l  w2s  o9l  w2s  o9l  w2s  o9l  w2s  o9l  w2s  o9l  w2s  o9l  w2s  o9l

e3d  i8k  e3d  i8k  e3d  i8k  e3d  i8k  e3d  i8k  e3d  i8k  e3d  i8k  e3d  i8k

r4f  u7j  r4f  u7j  r4f  u7j  r4f  u7j  r4f  u7j  r4f  u7j  r4f  u7j  r4f  u7j

t5g  y6h  t5g  y6h  t5g  y6h  t5g  y6h  t5g  y6h  t5g  y6h  t5g  y6h  t5g  y6h

w2s  o9l  e3d  i8k  r4f  u7j  t5g  y6h  w2s  o9l  e3d  i8k  r4f  u7j  t5g  y6h

1st  2nd  9th  3rd  8th  4th  7th  6th  1st  2nd  9th  3rd  8th  4th  7th  6th
```

Exercise 25

Margin stops: Pica 16 and 66; Elite 25 and 75

```
7th September, 1017; Canute was chosen as King.

3rd May, 1296; Scots lost the Battle of Dunbar.

18th March, 1455; the War of the Roses started.

22nd February, 1558; Calais captured by French.

5th November, 1605; Gunpowder Plots discovered.

8th September, 1704; English capture Gibraltar.

4th July, 1776; American Independence declared.

9th June, 1809; Sir John Moore died at Corunna.

31st May, 1902; peace with the Boers, Pretoria.

20th July, 1969; first man-landing on the moon.
```

Exercise 185

Display the contents page that follows, taking one carbon copy.

Exercise 186

Make a draft of the following information, listing the branches alphabetically by place. It is to be produced on a card measuring 5 × 7 in (12·7 × 17·8 cm).

CORNISH & LAMBERT LTD.

Head Office: 99 Bridge Street, London E13 9QD

Branches:		
	Wolverhampton WV6 0DD	Tudor House, Ford Street
	Liverpool L36 0SZ	74 Bourne Street
	Nottingham NG14 6AE	38 Gatehouse Lane
	Cardiff CF1 1DE	20 Waterhouse Street
	Edinburgh EH14 2HW	16 Melville Crescent
	Manchester M1 1PN	Deeside Mills, City Lane
	Leicester LE6 5DQ	8a Newbury Street
	Newcastle-upon-Tyne NE1 5JR	Kingsway, Tyne Valley Trading Estate
	Bournemouth BH8 0DP	59 Canford Road
	Bristol BS18 7ER	Queen's Road, Brillington Trading Estate
	Leeds LS17 6NE	78 Greenford Place
	Bath BA3 2PH	49 Kingsland Road

Exercise 26

They said their client would buy the stock (500 shares) at $9\frac{1}{2}\%$.

Ship the goods to Ceylon, per S.S. "Modena", at 90 days' sight.

They quote two-centimetre-mesh wire-netting @ £4.25 per roll.

"What is the price of coal?" he said, "I need 9 tonnes at once."

Messrs. J. Northcliffe & Co. sent me the following quotations:-

The order for laths 15 mm x 50 mm x 2 m was received on 2nd May.

£2.20 was the price quoted to you, but this is reduced to £2.15.

Exercise 27

Notice the use of the underscore for which the shift lock is used. *Do not* underscore final punctuation marks.

NOTICE IS HEREBY GIVEN that a DRAWING of BONDS of the THREE-AND-A-HALF-PER-CENT LOANS of 19-- took place on 26th June, when the following numbers were drawn for redemption:-

13 BONDS: Series B. Nos. 34560, 34561, 34562, 34563, 34564, 34565, 34566, 34567, 34568, 34569, 34570, 34571, 34572.

21 BONDS: Series C. Nos. 01234, 01235, 01236, 01237, 01238, 01239, 01240, 01241, 01242, 01243, 01244, 01245, 01246, 01247, 01248, 01249, 01250, 01251, 01252, 01253, 01254.

13 BONDS: Series D. Nos. 19870, 19871, 19872, 19873, 19874, 19875, 19876, 19877, 19878, 19879, 19880, 19881, 19882.

21 BONDS: Series E. Nos. 42700, 42701, 42702, 42703, 42704, 42705, 42706, 42707, 42708, 42709, 42710, 42711, 42712, 42713, 42714, 42715, 42716, 42717, 42718, 42719, 42720.

struck. Here are some examples of foreign words with accents; if necessary insert the accents in ink after typing the words:-

aún	españoles	über	spät	la différence	possède
también	niño	müde	öffnen	connaître	français

If accent keys are not fitted to the typewriter insert the accents neatly with a pen.

Exercise 182

The following exercise illustrates the use of the 24-hour clock—note that when typing the time no space occurs between the hours and minutes.

ITINERARY
(Mr. F. W. Browne)

Date and time of departure	Destination	Hotel
21 July 1420	Dep. Glasgow Airport Arr. Paris, Le Bourget	Hotel George V, 31 avenue George V, Paris 8ème.
23 July 1500	Dep. Paris, Le Bourget Arr. Luxembourg	Hotel Impérial, 68 rue de Napoléon, Luxembourg.
25 July 0830	Dep. Luxembourg Arr. Heidelberg (via Frankfurt Airport)	Hotel Krautheim, Königstrasse 27, Heidelberg.
28 July 1320	Dep. Cologne Arr. Glasgow Airport	

Exercise 183

On A5 paper make an alphabetical table in three columns of the information below. The third column is to be left blank for a specimen of the colour to be added.

HERALDIC COLOURS

The names of the heraldic colours are given below. It should be noted that one colour should not be superimposed on another nor one metal on the other.

Sable = black;   Gules = red;   Vert = green;   Purpure = purple
Azure = blue;   Or = gold (or yellow);   Argent = silver (or white)

Exercise 184

LIABILITIES TO THE PROPRIETORS

	Capital £	Reserves £	Balances £	Total £
1. Bank of Scotland	1,325,000	550,000	150,000	2,025,000
2. Royal	2,000,000	1,242,000	98,000	3,340,000
3. British Linen	1,250,000	1,350,000	98,000	2,698,000
4. Commercial	1,750,000	1,125,000	145,000	3,020,000
5. National	1,100,000	1,100,000	190,000	2,390,000
6. Union	1,000,000	1,000,000	218,000	2,218,000
7. Clydesdale	1,000,000	1,200,000	227,000	2,427,000
8. North of Scotland, etc.	652,000	652,000	222,000	1,526,000
Total for 19—	10,077,000	8,219,000	1,348,000	19,644,000
,, 19—	10,077,000	7,834,000	1,284,000	19,195,000
Increase in 19—	No change	385,000	64,000	449,000

Balanced Hand Sentences

In the following exercise the **first word is typed with the right hand and the second with the** left, and so on throughout the exercise. This affords practice in balanced hand movements.

Exercise 28

Margin stops: Pica 15 and 70; Elite 24 and 79

```
I gave him great joy, as I rewarded him at Hull.

Polly saw you at Pump Gate in Water Mill Street.

A Monopoly, as I feared John, added no zest in trade.

I gave you a minimum wage, Jim, as I saw you deserved.

Philip saw no trees in fact only grasses in a pool.
```

Balanced Finger Sentences

The following exercise is based on words in which **the right and left hands have to be used for alternate letters**. Before beginning to type any subsequent exercise you may turn back and type one of these sentences several times in order to loosen the finger joints.

Exercise 29

Margin stops: Pica 12 and 72; Elite 20 and 80

```
Jane may wish to pay the lame girl for the enamel ornament.

Dick is to fight when the eighty men go to the ancient city.

The field is to the right: do lend a hand and cut the corn.

Make a vow to quench fury and rid the air of fiendish envy.

The dismal man works with me when he is paid to do so.

Prod the fuel to make the shanty cosy for the girls.
```

MISCELLANEOUS EXERCISES

This section includes exercises of great variety. Many of them need a good deal of thought before you embark on the typing. Time yourself on these production-type jobs, so that you have some idea of your rate of output on work that is not straight copying. Your calculations must include time spent on planning the work, checking, making any necessary alterations and ruling up where required. Be especially careful when you are using ink; it is a waste of time to ruin good typing by careless ruling.

When you have finished the exercises given here, find others for yourself from newspapers and magazines. There is no end to the variety of work a good typist may be asked to do.

Exercise 181

Display the order form given below on A4 paper. Allow 1 in (25 mm) for letter head.

Name .... Membership No. ....

Address ....

....

Please send me the following books as ticked below:—

	Price	By Post
A.A. London Guide	62 p	67 p
Illustrated Road Book of England and Wales	£1·75	£1·90
Road Book of England and Wales	£1·25	£1·37
Illustrated Road Book of Scotland	£1·25	£1·37
Road Book of Scotland	87 p	95 p
Illustrated Road Book of Ireland	£1·25	£1·37
Road Book of Ireland	87 p	95 p
Fun on Wheels		
(stiff cloth cover)	42 p	47 p
(paper cover)	22 p	25 p
*Motorists—Know Your Law	17 p	20 p
Plastic Handbook Cover	13 p	16 p

*Not applicable to Ireland

I enclose cheque/postal order value ....

To facilitate dispatch, please write your name and address in BLOCK CAPITALS on the label below.

....

....

....

....

....

Dead Keys

Sometimes a typewriter is required for typing in foreign languages where certain accent signs are necessary. When a machine is to be used largely for foreign correspondence it should be fitted with the required accents and this can be done by dispensing with some other characters which are less likely to be required. If possible, the accents should be fitted to "dead" keys, i.e. keys which when struck do not cause the carriage to move forward: the accent key is struck first and then, without back spacing, the letter key is

Alphabetic Sentences

Each of the sentences in the following exercise contains all the letters of the alphabet. Before beginning to type any subsequent exercise you may turn back and type one of these sentences several times. Set a tabular stop at either 15 or 26 as appropriate for the following sentences, and use the tabulator to indent paragraphs.

Exercise 30

Margin stops: Pica 10 and 75; Elite 20 and 85

Swimming is an excellent and invigorating sport for health and enjoyment and it is amazing how quickly one can learn to be a good life-saver.

Jacqueline, who was very lazy, did not notice that the exercise had been worked before but May, who was a girl of wiser disposition, recognized it.

With extreme skill the youth quickly drove his fine car over the perilous bridge, knowing that one more narrow pass would end his amazing journey.

Crossing the neutral zone, I was attacked by snipers; and when jumping for cover I narrowly escaped exploding the bomb, and quaked with fear.

We gazed down upon the little fishing village, part of which was sheltered from winds by an extensive projecting rock, and which lay below in quiet peacefulness.

No noise disturbed the evening quiet of the wayside meadow as the unkempt prowler was joined by his zealous confederates, who were able to tell of excellent work.

Parts of India are covered with extensive jungles in which wild animals roam, and lizards dart quickly among the shrubs.

which shows the trading figures for the period January 1977 to January 1980. For the purposes of these proceedings I have had prepared by my said Accountants a schedule of future bookings & estimated receipts for the next nine months & this is now produced & shown to me marked "A.B.C.2"

5. In the premises I submit that my guest-house business is likely to run at a substantial profit in the foreseeable future & I request this Honourable Court, under its inherent jurisdiction, to allow me a further period of twelve months to continue my business at the expiry of which time I anticipate being able to pay off the arrears of interest under the said Charge & totalling £14,500 at the date hereof, & in the meantime I shall use my best endeavours to discharge current interest as it arises.

SWORN at   )
in the County of   )
)
this   day of   )

Before me,

A Solicitor empowered to
administer Oaths.

Paragraphs

Exercise 31

Margin stops: Pica 10 and 75; Elite 20 and 85

Each day we see terns and sea swallows playing round the
ship. They have not by any means come with us from the land.
They roam over the ocean and when they see our great ship they
sail close up to see if we are a rock or an island.

Exercise 32

Margin stops: Pica 10 and 75; Elite 20 and 85

In all worldly things that a man pursues with the greatest
eagerness and intention of mind imaginable, he finds not half
the pleasure in the actual possession of them as he proposed to
himself in the expectation.

Exercise 33

Margin stops: Pica 10 and 75; Elite 20 and 85

To live content with small means; to seek elegance rather
than luxury, and refinement rather than fashion; to be worthy,
not respectable, and wealthy, not rich; to listen to stars and
birds, babes and sages with open heart; to study hard; to think
quietly, act frankly, talk gently, await occasions, hurry never;
in a word, to let the spiritual, unbidden and unconscious, grow
up through the common - this is my symphony.

Type one copy of the following Affidavit.

1980 No 1234

IN THE HIGH COURT OF JUSTICE
CHANCERY DIVISION
GROUP C

BETWEEN

SHARK (MORTGAGEES) LIMITED

Plaintiffs

-and-

AVERY POORMAN

Defendant

I, AVERY POORMAN of Blackacre, Snooks Road in the County of Wessex, guest-house proprietor, MAKE OATH and SAY as follows:—

1. I am the Defendant in this action. The facts hereinafter stated are within my knowledge.

2. By Legal Charge dated the 29th day of February 1976 the Plaintiffs lent to me a sum of £50,000 at an annual rate of interest of 20 per centum per annum for 25 years. I utilized the said principal sum to purchase the property Blackacre, Snooks Road, aforesaid. The said property comprises five double and five single bedrooms, a restaurant seating 25 persons, a reception and a recreation area.

3. Between February 1976 and January 1977 I spent a total of £15,000 on improvements to the said property converting it from a residential detached house to a boarding house which since the latter date I have run as a business venture taking in guests throughout the summer periods.

4. Substantial profits in a venture of this kind cannot be expected in the first few years. I verily believe that profits can be made within the next year. There is now produced and shown to me marked "A.B.C.1" a profit & loss account produced by my Accountants Messrs. Overcharge & Co

This exercise is continued on page 92.

Word Division

The following exercises are set in printer's type. When you are typing these exercises, you will find that it is sometimes necessary to divide words with hyphens at the ends of lines, in order to keep the right-hand margin as even as possible. Read the following rules carefully:—

1. Words should be divided whenever possible into syllables, but a syllable of one letter should not be left at the end of a line, nor should a syllable of two letters be carried forward.

2. Composite words should be divided into their original parts, for example, school-master, mantel-piece, bag-pipe.

3. Words containing a hyphen should be divided at the point of the hyphen, for example, co-operative, gate-keeper.

4. Words containing double letters are usually divided at the point between the double letters, for example, syl-lable, com-mission, gut-ter.

5. Words of one syllable and their plurals should not be divided.

6. You should avoid dividing a date, or typing a courtesy title at the end of the line and the name on the next line.

7. Proper nouns should not be divided.

If you need to type characters beyond the point set for the right-hand margin, it is possible to do so by releasing the margin by depressing the margin-release key.

You should avoid dividing words on two consecutive lines and having more than two or three line-end divisions to each paragraph.

Margin stops: Pica 10 and 75; Elite 20 and 85
Line-space lever for double-line spacing

Exercise 34
Good health is a factor in success. No man can reach the limit of his power unless he is well and happy, and it is as great a sin to neglect the body as it is to omit to develop the mind. It is much easier to keep well by giving due thought to the natural laws of health than it is to get well when once a careless or a bad habit has been allowed to work its will and lower the physical standard. The state of the mind and the state of the body react upon each other.

(470 strokes = 94 words)

Exercise 35
Up to now the material used for flexible office records has been card as distinct from paper, because the record has a lasting value; but there is another aspect to be considered. While in theory the record will exist as long as the firm does, the card will not be handled all that time. Some cards will fill up quickly and be transferred after a short period. It is therefore wasteful to use for twenty weeks a form of a quality that would last for twenty years.

(464 strokes = 93 words)

Exercise 36
Wisdom is not born with us. It is a plant of slow growth, and old men have at least had more time to grow wise. They have lived longer, and they have learned more. And it is with old books as with old men. There are few of us who do not look back with regret upon the time we wasted in reading second-rate modern books because there was no wise friend to guide us. What a pity someone did not point out to us that really good writers had said the same things before, and said them better.

(492 strokes = 98 words)

Exercise 37
The human voice is one of the simplest devices of Nature, and yet it is one of the most mysterious. By the aid of a fine voice with its wide range of tone a man or woman may exert a very great charm. Yet who can explain why one voice pleases and another fails to do so? It is in the first place a question of timbre and the shape of the voice-box or larynx. That, however, is not the end of the subject, for there is probably no other faculty that may be so greatly improved by training.

(494 strokes = 99 words)

Exercise 38
A sense of humour is one of the most precious gifts. It is as oil to the wheels of life. There is little hope for the man who is gloomy, and who cannot see the funny side of the tiresome little events of every day. He it is who will meet troubles half-way and spend the energy he needs today in fighting the foes of tomorrow, which he may never see. Many people have white hairs caused by troubles that have never come. Laughter keeps the mind and body young. A happy doctor does more good than his medicine.

(513 strokes = 103 words)

Exercise 39
Let me say this to you. Be keen to do your best whether you succeed or fail. If you succeed, you will have the pleasure of your success. If you fail, you will know your failure does not arise through any fault of yours. Your future is in your own hands. Try in settling your vocation in life to think that it will be not only your work but your pleasure. The struggle for existence and success is so great nowadays that those who tackle their work in a perfunctory manner have no chance of reaching their goal.

(516 strokes = 103 words)

Exercise 179

The following exercise is a will. Notice the way in which it is displayed. Pay particular attention to the attestation clause, which differs slightly from the one shown on page 88.

THIS IS THE LAST WILL AND TESTAMENT of me JOHN SMITH of———

35 High Street Kingston Upon Hull in the East Riding of the——

County of Yorkshire Grocer————————————————

WHEREBY:—————————————————————

      I REVOKE all former Wills and Codicils made by me at——

any time—————————————————————————

      I APPOINT my wife Jessie Smith to be the sole executrix

of this my Will——————————————————————

      I BEQUEATH to my brother Samuel Smith of Chanctonbury——

Farm Long Barrow Hill Cirencester in the County of—————

Gloucestershire my gold pocket watch and my collection of——

seven oil paintings free of any duties payable on and by——

reason of my death—————————————————————

      I GIVE DEVISE AND BEQUEATH all the residue of my estate

both real and personal unto my wife the said Jessie Smith——

absolutely and I DIRECT her to pay thereout all my just debts

and funeral and testamentary expenses———————————

      IN WITNESS whereof I have hereunto set my hand this——

THIRTIETH day of MAY One thousand nine hundred and seventy——

```
SIGNED by John Smith of 35 High  )
Street Kingston Upon Hull as his  )
last Will in the presence of us   )
present at the same time who at    )
his request in his presence and   )
in the presence of each other     )
have subscribed our names as       )
attesting witnesses                )
```

Exercise 40

Sound buying is an essential to the success of a trading concern. Any sale that may be made implies a certain amount of buying in order to provide that which is needed to supply the demand made for the products. The degree of business acumen shown in this buying has a very definite effect on the net profit that will be shown when the transaction is carried through. Orders are as good as worthless if the Purchases Section so far falls below the standard expected of it as to buy in a bad market or to fail to secure prompt delivery. *(538 strokes = 108 words)*

Exercise 41

Business men often fail because they do not know how to handle men. They can do their own work all right, but they fail when it comes to directing others. They lack tact and patience. They lose their temper over little things, and no man is a good leader who cannot control himself. In giving way to ill temper he forfeits the respect of those in his presence, and this is fatal. Some men think that to get the best out of their employees they must drive, and scold, and find fault. The best leader is quiet, kind, and courteous. *(535 strokes = 107 words)*

Exercise 42

A good memory is a business asset. It saves energy, time and money. To give one's whole mind to the task in hand is the best way to strengthen a weak memory. People rarely forget facts that concern them very nearly and matters in which they take a deep, personal interest. This principle may be applied in the business office, and the typist who desires to increase her value will save many a journey to the filing room and many a hunt for information by retaining in her mind the substance of the letters she is called upon to type. *(536 strokes = 107 words)*

Exercise 43

Hard work is the surest way to success in life, and almost any man who has achieved greatness will admit that he had to toil without ceasing in order that he might get to the high places. The reward is sometimes slow in coming. Carlyle was practically unknown at the age of forty-five. Everything worth doing takes time and it is out of defeat and failure that success comes. Many a famous novelist looks back upon the time when his first novel was completed only to be rejected again and again by men who did not recognize its merit. *(538 strokes = 108 words)*

Exercise 44

Various methods have been evolved for keeping summaries of records in a form that makes consultation easy. This is usually done by means of cards. Sometimes these serve merely as an index, directing the searcher to the original documents or books. Sometimes the cards contain important information extracted from the original records in a form that summarizes the history of the matter. Apart from the uses of cards as an index, sometimes the original record itself is kept on cards. *(492 strokes = 98 words)*

Exercise 45

There is a growing class of people known as advertisement writers, who furnish ideas for advertising agents or traders, and undoubtedly what may be termed the art of advertisement writing had been seriously cultivated by many people during the past years. Whilst a serious study of advertising may produce an improved organization and method, it may produce little in the way of a striking advertisement, because the imagination so necessary in such a case is a characteristic with which not everyone is gifted. *(481 strokes = 96 words)*

Figures and Abbreviations

Margin stops: Pica 10 and 75; Elite 20 and 85
Line-space lever for double-line spacing

Exercise 46

There is general agreement that the size of women's feet has increased in recent years. Fifteen or twenty years ago 4s and 5s were the sizes most in demand, with a proportion of 3s, and even a 2 was not uncommon. But the increase amounts only to about one size. I have before me a factor's current list in which women's shoes are quoted as 3–8, from which it appears that 3s can still be obtained in the ordinary sizes, but that 9 is regarded as an outsize. *(464 strokes = 93 words)*

Exercise 47

The S.S. "Speedaway," having a carrying capacity of 4,050 tonnes and passenger accommodation for about 44 first- and second-class travellers, has been successfully launched at Amsterdam. The ship has the following dimensions: 117 metres by 15 metres by 9 metres; and has a draught of 6 metres. The triple expansion engines give 3,150 h.p. which will give the ship a speed of $12\frac{1}{4}$ knots. The new steamer is owned by Messrs. Bindle & Coates, and will shortly be placed on the Europe to Indonesia route. *(517 strokes = 103 words)*

Exercise 178

The following exercise is a memorandum of agreement. Notice the way in which it is set out and type one copy of it.

THIS AGREEMENT made this ELEVENTH day of MAY in —— the year One thousand nine hundred and seventy-six BETWEEN—— MIRIAM ACTON of 36 Chestnut Drive Southport in the County of—— Lancashire (hereinafter called "the Employee") of the one part—— and ROBERT PLESTED of Tunnel House Southport in the County of—— Lancashire (hereinafter called "the Employer") of the other part— WHEREBY IT IS AGREED that ———————————————————————

1. THE Employer hereby appoints the Employee (who hereby accepts— the appointment) as a full-time member of the secretarial staff—— at Tunnel House Southport in the County of Lancashire on and from— the FIRST day of OCTOBER One thousand nine hundred and seventy-six

2. THE commencing salary to be Forty Pounds per week——————————

3. EXCEPT in respect of a period during which the Employee is—— absent from work owing to illness injury or other disability and— except in so far as this Agreement may otherwise provide the—— Employer shall pay to the Employee as from the date of her——— appointment a salary payable under and in accordance with the—— scale applicable to the appointment hereby made ————————

4. IF the Employee gives or is given notice to terminate her—— employment in accordance with the provisions of this Agreement—— then the said notice becomes effective at the end of four clear— weeks—————————————————————————————————————

5. THE books of the firm are the property of ROBERT PLESTED and— the Employee shall not during the engagement remove any of the—— books or divulge the contents thereof to anyone not so connected— with the business——————————————————————————————

AS WITNESS THE HANDS OF THE PARTIES the said MIRIAM ACTON and the said ROBERT PLESTED the day and year first above written———————————— in the presence of

.... Witness   .... Employer's
                                                                        Signature

.... Witness   .... Employee's
                                                                        Signature

Exercise 48

After paying interest on mortgages, repairs and renewals, directors' remuneration, and income tax, there remains a balance of £26,507.21, which your directors propose to deal with as follows: nine months' dividend on Preference shares to 31st October, already paid, £6,300; Preference dividend accrued to 31st January, £2,100; dividend at the rate of 4p per share on the Ordinary shares for six months to 31st July, tax free, already paid, £3,750; dividend at the rate of 6p per share on the Ordinary shares for six months to 31st January, making a total distribution of 10p per share for the year, tax free, £6,250; and balance to next account £8,107.21.   *(641 strokes = 128 words)*

Exercise 49

Claims paid, including provision for outstanding losses, amounted to £3,710,178, being 59·4 per cent of the premium income and 58·5 per cent of the premiums earned during the year. Commission to agents, expenses of management, alterations and repairs, and every expense outgo exclusive of taxes, amounted to £2,297,132, being 35·7 per cent of the premium income. In taxes, including income tax deducted at the source, the Corporation paid £221,907, equal to 3·5 per cent of the premium income. This compares with £223,002, being 3·3 per cent in the previous year. After making the necessary provision for unearned premiums, there remained an underwriting profit of £240,490.

(681 strokes = 136 words)

Punctuation Marks—II

The following exercises give additional practice in the use of punctuation marks.

Notice the use of single quotation marks for quotations within a quotation. If a quotation occupies more than one paragraph, type the quotation marks at the beginning of each paragraph, and at the end of the final paragraph.

Use the hyphen, with a space before and after it, to represent the dash.

If your machine does not contain a sign for the exclamation mark type an apostrophe, backspace once, and then type the full stop.

Margin stops: Pica 10 and 75; Elite 20 and 85
Line-space lever for double-line spacing

Exercise 50

"Watch yourself closely whenever you are tempted to use such words as 'case,' 'instance,' 'character,' 'condition,' 'like.' 'Train your suspicions to bristle up,' says Sir Arthur Quiller-Couch, 'whenever you come upon "as regards," "with regard to," "according as to whether," and the like. You should never use them.' "

Exercise 52

" 'Nightingales?' I asked, breathlessly.

" 'Aye, but it's quiet down here!' my companion sighed. 'Maybe when we start broadcasting or listening-in the old place will wake up a bit and life will become tolerable!'

" 'You are a thousand years ahead of some of us in that respect,' I said, with enthusiasm. 'I mean at broadcasting. . . .'

" 'Joking, aren't you?' asked the steward.

" 'But surely you have spent evening after evening listening-in?' I queried.

" 'What to?' my companion asked, brusquely.

" 'The nightingales!' I replied, promptly."— Donald Grant.

Exercise 51

On opening my eyes, the first thing that meets them is my own breath rolling forth, as if in the open air, like smoke out of a cottage chimney. Think of this symptom. Then I turn my eyes sideways and see the window all frozen over. Think of that. Then the servant comes in. "It is very cold this morning, is it not?"—"Very cold, Sir."—"Very cold indeed, isn't it?"—"Very cold indeed, Sir."—"More than usually so, isn't it, even for this weather?" (Here the servant's wit and good nature are put to a considerable test, and the inquirer lies on thorns for the answer.) "Why, Sir . . . I think it is." (Good creature! There is not a better, or more truth-telling servant going.) "I must rise, however—get me some warm water."—Here comes a fine interval between the departure of the servant and the arrival of the hot water; during which, of course, it is of "no use" to get up. The hot water comes. "Is it quite hot?"—"Yes, Sir."— "Perhaps too hot for shaving: I must wait a little?"—"No, Sir. It will just do." (There is an over-nice propriety sometimes, an officious zeal of virtue.)

LEGAL WORK

Legal work differs in some respects from ordinary commercial work. In legal documents, punctuation is omitted, unless the document contains numbered clauses, when a full stop is typed at the end of each clause. The beginning of a new sentence is generally indicated by a space preceding it, and by the typing of the first letter or word in capital letters.

The names of the parties and other important words are typed in capital letters, and words such as AGREEMENT, THIS CONVEYANCE, IN WITNESS, are typed in spaced capitals.

No abbreviations should be used; words should not be divided at the ends of lines; and all numbers, except the numbers of houses and of postal districts, should be expressed in words.

A black record ribbon is normally used, and no erasure may be made.

Many legal documents are prepared in the first instance in the form of a draft. Drafts are typed in treble-line spacing, with wide margins, so that alterations and additions can be made easily. The word "Draft" should be typed at the head of each sheet of paper.

The attestation clause should be typed so that it extends about half an inch into the left-hand margin, and the following is the normal form of display:—

```
SIGNED SEALED AND DELIVERED)
by the said Eliza Benson    )
in the presence of          )
```

Endorsements

Legal documents are usually folded into four, as shown in the illustration. Notice the way in which the endorsement is set out in this illustration. To type an endorsement, fold the document into four, and then open it out again so that it is folded into two, and insert it into the typewriter with the middle crease on the right. The endorsement is then typed on the right-hand side, and the document afterwards refolded.

Dated 16th September, 19--

Wilfred Birdsall
& Co. Ltd.

and

William Robert Perkins, Esq.

—————

A G R E E M E N T

for sale of Freehold House at
242 Ragland Road, Croydon

—————

Gordon Smith & Son,
1 Parkinson Gate,
London
W1V 4NA

Copying Skill Development

The following exercises provide practice in straightforward copying. Exercises 53 to 58 are copying tests set by the Royal Society of Arts. The speed can be checked at any time by dividing the number of strokes typed by five (to find the number of words typed), and then dividing the answer by the number of minutes taken to type the exercise (to find the speed in words per minute). Remember to type carefully as accuracy is more important than speed.

For the following exercises set the margin stops at 10 and 75 (Pica) or 20 and 85 (Elite), and the line-space lever for double-line spacing.

Exercise 53

	Strokes
The management of a factory can be one of the most fascinating	63
occupations. It provides ample scope for the whole variety of human	132
characteristics and yields rewards for skill and perseverance not easily to	208
be reaped elsewhere. There is a satisfaction to be experienced in creating	284
something tangible, useful, and attractive from the most ordinary raw	354
materials; a mental exhilaration accompanying the technical development	426
of a most complex and astonishing device starting from a blank sheet of	498
paper; and a thrill in seeing in movement a machine which has lived for	570
months only in the minds of its builders. No general launching of a	639
campaign is to be envied by a man embarking on the production of a new	710
article. A scientist finding at last the new material of perhaps arresting	786
beauty, though derived from coal-tar and sawdust, has no more reason	855
to feel satisfied than the manufacturer who picks up that material, has its	931
properties tabulated, and its potentialities analysed, and then creates from	1008
it an article attractive, ingenious, and useful.	1056

(211 *words*)

Exercise 54

	Strokes
From the point of view of the audience effective platform work seems	69
remarkably easy. It is just the apparent simplicity of its performance	141
which is the hall-mark of its perfection as an art. Indeed, simplicity is the	220
basis of all art.	238
Simplicity in itself is not always a quality that it is easy to attain.	310
There are so many other effects which attract attention, and this is	380
especially so when we consider the appeal which a speaker makes to his	451
audience. All speakers have their own particular characteristics, their	524
own little tricks of speech, their own little idiosyncrasies of gesture; but,	602
in determining the speakers who make the most pleasing appeal to you,	672
you will invariably find that they are those who express themselves simply,	748
who do not lead your attention down the by-ways of involved rhetoric,	818
into a morass of words that convey no clear idea to you.	875
How do these speakers achieve this ease of expression, this gift of	943
holding the attention of an audience for an hour at a time with no apparent	1019
effort? The one great secret is: preparation.	1066

(213 *words*)

Take three carbon copies of this exercise.

MOTOR CARS

Anti-Frost Precautions

To avoid damage by frost, it is desirable to employ in the cooling system a mixture of water & pure glycerine or methylated spirit in the following proportions :—

u.c.

Capacity of Cooling System	Mixture to Withstand 20° of frost		Mixture to Withstand 32° of frost	
	Water	Pure glycerine or Meth. Spirit	Water	Pure Glycerine or Meth. Spirit
Litres	Litres	Litres	Litres	Litres
5	$3\frac{1}{2}$	$1\frac{1}{2}$	3	2
6	4	2	$3\frac{1}{2}$	$2\frac{1}{2}$
7	$4\frac{3}{4}$	$2\frac{1}{4}$	4	3
8	$5\frac{1}{2}$	$2\frac{1}{2}$	$4\frac{3}{4}$	$3\frac{1}{2}$
9	$6\frac{1}{4}$	$2\frac{3}{4}$	$5\frac{1}{4}$	$3\frac{3}{4}$
10	7	3	6	4
11	$7\frac{1}{2}$	$3\frac{1}{2}$	$6\frac{1}{2}$	$4\frac{1}{2}$
13	9	4	9	6
15	$10\frac{1}{2}$	$4\frac{1}{2}$	$7\frac{3}{4}$	$5\frac{1}{4}$

l.c. Crude glycerine shd. not be used. Glycerine does not evaporate — the cooling system may be replenished with water only.

Exercise 55

When drafting any advertisement, care should be taken to state clearly 71
what is required. Here is an example of a good advertisement for computer 145
programmers. 158

"Linear programming models play an important and highly profitable 225
role in this Company and the expansion of our linear programming teams 296
is being given top priority. These teams exist in most operating Divisions 373
where they are responsible to informed management for formulating and 443
solving a wide range of applications in production scheduling, in distribu- 518
tion planning and for long-term capital projects. These Divisional teams 591
are supported by a central group with special responsibility for program- 664
ming systems, formulation techniques and development. 717

"Several positions are available in the Divisional teams and in the central 793
group for men with linear programming experience of at least one year, 865
but preferably longer. This experience may be in the formulation and 934
solution of large new problems, in the operation of routine application 1105
systems or in more theoretical work and computer programme development. 1176
The rapid development of linear programming and the wide knowledge 1243
of Company activities which work in this field engenders will provide 1313
outstanding career prospects for the right men." 1362

(*272 words*)

Exercise 56

In every firm it should be recognized as an invariable rule that no 68
clerk should remain in possession of original letters. All correspondence 143
which cannot be dealt with within forty-eight hours should be returned 214
to the manager. 229

A letter which, from its nature, requires a longer time for reply (as, for 304
instance, where an inquiry has first to be made, or where a certain date 377
has to be awaited) must receive particular attention. The clerk dealing 450
with it should make a note in a book to remind him of the letter, or some 524
other mechanical device should be adopted to ensure that the letter does not 601
remain unattended to when circumstances are sufficiently developed to 671
permit further action. 694

A deviation from the general rule of answering or attending to every 763
letter immediately upon receipt is made by those firms who, owing to 832
external circumstances, can dispatch only on certain days of the week 902
or month, as for instance agents and booksellers, who dispatch publications 978
on the date of issue. 999

In the export business, use has to be made of vessels which sail on 1067
pre-arranged days of the month, so that the dates of departure must be 1138
taken into consideration when dealing with the correspondence. 1200

(*240 words*)

Typist — The drugs should
be listed alphabetically

Butazolidin   Eases rheumatic aches. Used
when aspirin fails.

Telmid   A blue dye which kills a
wide range of human intes-
tinal worms, when other drugs
fail. Also rids cats and dogs
of the roundworms that can
cause blindness when caught
by children.

Portyn.   Helps peptic ulcers to heal by
repressing the movements of
the stomach and intestines.

Dytide   2 different drugs which drain
surplus fluid out of the tissues
bloated by heart disease.

Drinamyl
(Spansule)   Prolonged-action version of what
were called "Purple Hearts." Like
the tablets they contain a barbi-
turate and a stimulant, widely
prescribed together to cure anxiety
without causing drowsiness.

Feospan   A new, one-dose-a-day method of
taking iron for the correction of simple anaemia.

Strokes

Those who think that money will not be needed in the highly socialized   70
states of the future are thinking in Utopian terms.   Money is even more   146
necessary in a communistic state than in a capitalistic state.   It is, and   223
always will be, the broad highway of economic exchanges.   Its services as   297
a means of exchange will be as necessary to all as are those of the great   371
arterial roads, but there will be restrictions on its use as a store of wealth.   450

Economic thought is moving along the lines of becoming more the study   523
of the efforts of man to secure a high standard of living in the world of   597
actuality than the study of a world of so-called "real" wealth with money   673
only as a subsidiary.   Rather is it the tendency now to regard money as   746
the most liquid form of wealth, and to look upon the rate of interest as   819
being the price of this liquidity, than to regard interest as the price of   894
loanable concrete capital.   920

So, economists cannot—as such—regard money as being an evil, not   992
even a necessary one, nor can they regard the love of money as being the   1065
root of all evil, for money is a very useful economic device, and is loved   1140
because of that usefulness.   Its real functions have not been known to the   1216
man in the street until recent years, mainly because there has always been   1291
a political taint attaching to writers who lay bare the real meaning of   1363
finance.   Gradually, however, the facts are becoming common knowledge   1432
and citizens of the future will, if they are wise, see to it that money is   1509
subordinated from being master to being servant.   1557

We must always remember that, under a system of private enterprise,   1628
the personal and geographical distribution of goods, and the balancing of   1702
production and consumption, are brought about by changes in money   1768
prices dictated by the relative movements of supply and demand.   1831

(366 *words*)

Footnotes

Footnote signs appear above the line of typing: see p. 52 for typing instructions. Most typewriters now have an upper-case character for the asterisk. In the text, leave no space between the footnote sign and the preceding character, but in the footnote itself, leave one space between the sign and the first word.

Footnotes are typed in single spacing with double spacing between them. A line extending the width of the typewritten matter is typed below the text and the first footnote should be typed two line spaces beneath it.

Take care to leave enough space at the bottom of the page for the footnote(s).

Exercise 175

It was in the year 1942 that, in conjunction with Dr. H. V. Wheeler (now Professor of Fuel Technology at Sheffield University), I began systematically to investigate as a fundamental problem the accelerating influence of hot surfaces upon combustion* And as the subsequent technical developments have been based upon principles discovered or elucidated during a series of scientific researches carried out under my direction by a succession of skilled collaborators[I] during the past twenty years, I think it right to draw attention to what I consider the more important features of our work.

By the year 1947 I had succeeded in proving (1) That at temperatures below the ignition point all hot surfaces have the power of accelerating gaseous combustion in varying degrees according to their chemical character and physical texture; (2) That whenever a mixture of combustible gas and oxygen (or air) is combining in contact with such a hot surface, the chemical action mainly occurs in, and is usually confined to, the boundary layers between the gaseous and solid phases wherever these may be in contact; and (3) that not only does the accelerating influence of a hot

* For this early work vide PHIL. TRANS. ROY. SOC. (1945) A202 pp. 1-7.
[I] Dr. H. Hartley, Messrs G. W. Andrew, A. Forshaw, A. Robson + others

Strokes

Many graces known in the less hurried past have been lost in the | 66
hurly-burly of our modern way of life. Gone is the courtliness once part of | 145
daily social intercourse; much of the dignity formerly associated with | 216
dining has passed to the limbo; and many of the gracious courtesies | 283
observed by our grandfathers have become little more than meaningless | 353
gestures. | 362

Our modern method of dealing with private correspondence is just | 430
one example of the change in social customs. Today, it is not thought | 502
necessary by many to fulfil the old-time obligation to send a note acknow- | 575
ledging a favour conferred or expressing a sense of pleasure enjoyed during | 651
a visit to a friend. If, perchance, the thought does occur, the obligation | 727
is quite likely to be discharged through the medium of the telephone or | 800
by a note dictated and written on a typewriter. | 847

Apropos of the use of a typewriter for this, we recall an incident | 917
quoted in the "Christian Science Monitor." During a visit to the Southern | 998
United States, a man from Massachusetts (in the Northern States) became | 1077
acquainted with one of the courtly old planters who are typical of the | 1148
South. On returning home, the Massachusetts man received a letter from | 1223
the old planter. The envelope contained a letter and a typewritten | 1292
enclosure. He naturally turned to the letter first, and it began: "Out of | 1370
courtesy to you I write in my own hand, but, to save your time and to | 1441
spare you the annoyance of deciphering it, I also send a typewritten copy | 1516
which I have prepared for you." | 1549

Writing a letter in bygone days was no small matter. There were | 1621
no such conveniences as the ball-point pen, while blotting-paper and | 1690
gummed envelopes were equally unknown. The equipment was the | 1753
"standish" or inkstand with its various accessories. | 1807

(361 *words*)

Type the following extract in double-line spacing with margins of $1\frac{1}{2}$ in (18 mm) on the left and 1 in (25 mm) on the right.

The length of the bridge & its approaches is about 180 m, making it one of the largest reinforced concrete structures of its class in the kingdom. The width is 12·5 m between parapets, providing a roadway of 8·25 m & two footpaths, each 2 m wide. The roadway over the arch has a gradient of 1 in 30, as in the case of the approaches. The river arch has a rise of 6 m above normal water level. [The main arch has fan ribs, those outside being 1,220 mm wide by 1,422 mm deep at the springings & 1,069 mm deep at the crown, while the two inner ribs are 1,400 mm wide and the same depth as the two outer ribs. Above each rib are two series of spandrel columns, 254 mm by 610 mm in cross-section, one series starting from the (northern) and the other from the (southern) abutments. The columns, spaced 1·5 m apart longitudinally, support longitudinal main beams, 250 mm wide by 500 mm deep, apart from the 188 mm decking slab. These beams are connected by transverse secondary beams, spaced 1·5 m apart longitudinally, and measuring 177 mm wide by 354 mm deep, apart from the thickness of the decking slab. The latter extends over and is incorporated with the two series of beams, to which it acts as a common compression flange.

N.P.

84

LETTER WRITING

The following exercises give practice in the typing of letters. The layout of business letters is largely a matter of individual preference, and practice varies with different firms. The following notes are for guidance.

LETTER-HEADINGS. Most business firms use printed letter-headings, giving the name and address of the firm, the nature of the business, the telephone and Telex numbers, and other relevant information. The size of the paper used varies considerably with different firms. Common sizes are International A4 (210 × 298 mm), and International A5 (210 × 149 mm).

MARGINS. The width of the margins usually varies according to the size of paper and length of letter, but sometimes it is predetermined by an alignment with the letter-heading.

REFERENCES. The reference may consist of the initials of the dictator and the typist (HT/JB), or of a departmental file number (ADV/51). The purpose of the reference is to identify the department issuing the letter. The reference is usually placed directly beneath the printed letter-heading. It should not extend into the left-hand margin. When replying to a letter in which a reference has been quoted, type the reference of your correspondent first, followed by your own reference, as in Exercise 60.

Some firms include a space for the reference in their printed letter-heading.

DATE. The date is usually typed immediately below the printed letter-heading. It should not extend into the right-hand margin. It is generally typed in the order of day, month, year, as 10*th* *May*, 19—.

ADDRESSEE. The name and address of the person to whom you are writing (the addressee) is typed at the left-hand side of the letter. Single-line spacing is used, even if the body of the letter is typed in double-line spacing.

Messrs. should be used when addressing a partnership, except when the name of the firm is preceded by the word *The*, or a title is included. Examples are *Messrs. Aldous & Co.; Messrs. Black & White; The Graham Manufacturing Co.; Sir John Brown & Co.*

A limited company is an incorporated body—a legal person, distinct from any of its members. Therefore *Messrs.* should not be used before the name of a limited company. When writing to a limited company, address the letter to *The Secretary*, or to some other official of the company—

for example, *The General Manager.*

SALUTATION. Common forms in business are *Dear Sir*, *Dear Madam*, *Sir*, *Sirs*, *Gentlemen*. The salutation should be flush with the left-hand margin, usually three line spaces below the inside address. It should be followed by a comma.

BODY OF THE LETTER. The body of the letter may be typed in single- or double-line spacing. Double-line spacing is always used between paragraphs. The first line of each paragraph may be indented, as in Exercise 60, five spaces from the left-hand margin (six when using elite type); or the block method may be used, as in Exercise 61.

COMPLIMENTARY CLOSE. Common forms used in business are *Yours faithfully*, *Yours truly*, and *Yours sincerely*. The complimentary close is generally typed two line spaces below the body of the letter. It is usually centred on the body of the letter, or placed so that it begins at the centre of the body of the letter.

NAME OF THE FIRM. Frequently the name of the firm is typed in capital letters immediately below the complimentary close. It is usually either centred on the complimentary close or it begins at the same point.

DESIGNATION. The designation of the person signing the letter is often included. It is usually centred on or aligned with the complimentary close, or it may be placed so that it finishes slightly to the right of the complimentary close or flush with the right-hand margin. Several line spaces should be left above it to leave room for the signature.

ENCLOSURES. Enclosures may be indicated by abbreviated forms Enc. or Encs. typed flush with the left-hand margin, a few spaces below the designation, or by typing a line of three dots or three hyphens in the left-hand margin against the line in which mention of the enclosure is made. Sometimes stick-on "enclosure" labels are affixed.

ERASING OF ERRORS.—Errors may be corrected by means of an eraser. Move the carriage to the side so that the eraser dust does not fall in the machine. Turn up the cylinder three or four spaces and gently erase the error. Blow the eraser dust away from the machine and return the work to the printing position for typing.

Exercise 172

SPECIFICATION and Schedule for alterations and additions to Electric-light Installation at Nos. 226–8 Railton Street, London E7 8NG, to be carried out to the entire satisfaction of

Messrs. Nelson, Carter & Sons,
Architects,
District Chambers,
London E7 8NG

March, 19—

GENERAL CONDITIONS

(1) The whole of the work set out in this Specification, Schedule and Drawing to be carried out so as to form an absolutely complete Electric-light Installation, and all such work that may be fairly implied from the specification, drawing or schedule to be included although some may not be specially mentioned.

(2) The Contractor to provide all essential tools and plant and give all necessary personal supervision, leaving a competent man to carry out the installation.

(3) The work to be put in hand immediately upon receipt of order, and completed to the specified time, but the Contractor is not to charge for any delays which may occur during the progress of the work due to non-completion of building or other unforeseen causes.

(4) All accidental or intentional damage to the building by Contractor's employees must be made good at his expense. He must also cover himself against loss by fire or water.

(5) No additional work to be put in hand without an order signed by the Architect and only upon such orders will payment be made.

(6) The installation to be completed to the entire approval of the Architect, and it must also meet the requirements and tests of the Insurance Co. and Supply Co. concerned. The Architect will have power to reject any unsatisfactory work or materials.

(7) The Contractor to guarantee his work for six months from time of completion and to make good, at his own expense, any faults which may develop though the work may previously have been passed.

(8) Payment will be made through the Builders, Messrs. Shaw & Curwin, up to 90% of the value of the work done.

1st payment on completion of the installation. 2nd payment of 10% outstanding balance three months after completion providing no faults develop in the meantime.

Exercise 173

Display the following specification. Take four carbon copies. Check your typing with care before removing it from the typewriter. The figures are particularly important in technical work.

Address an envelope of suitable size or cut paper to envelope size. The name of the firm is Harman & Jones Ltd. Remember to insert a post code on the envelope. Fold the specification for insertion into the envelope of your choice.

SPECIFICATION and Schedule for supplying, delivering and erecting Industrial Steel Shelving at 341–9 Great West Road, Brentford, Middx.

July, 19—

TO THE SUPPLY, DELIVERY AND ERECTION OF:

Industrial Steel Shelving, comprising:–
2 Single Faced Static Units, 2,900 × 4,600 mm long × 457 mm deep, having solid backs and sides, top, bottom and 8 Intermediate Shelves.

8 Double Faced Units, 2,900 mm high × 1,800 mm overall length × 762 mm overall depth (481 mm each face), having solid backs and sides, top, bottom and 8 Intermediate Shelves.

7 Double Faced Units, 2,900 mm high × 1,800 mm overall length × 610 mm overall depth (305 mm each face), having solid backs and sides, top, bottom and 8 Intermediate Shelves.

2 Double Faced Units, 2,900 mm high × 1,800 mm overall length × 915 mm deep overall (457 mm each face), having solid backs and sides, top, bottom and 8 Intermediate Shelves.

One Double Faced Unit, 2,900 mm high × 1,800 mm long × 610 mm overall depth, having solid backs and sides, top, bottom and 10 Intermediate Shelves. Bottom 2 shelves in all units to be on 305 mm centres, with next 4 on 152 mm centres, complete with one divider, next 5 on 305 mm centres.

FOR THE SUM OF: £1,745

FINISH: Shelving—bonderised stove enamel dove grey.

DELIVERY: Shelving—six weeks from receipt of official order.
Partitioning—six weeks from approval of working drawings.

TERMS: Nett 30 days. The above prices are based on the present day ruling prices of raw materials.

INDENTED style—First line of each paragraph is indented.
Margin stops: Pica 12 and 72; Elite 20 and 80
Tab. stops: 17 or 26

Notice that one space is left between the two parts of the post code
which forms the last line of the address.

DKJ/ER   15th May, 19--

Compton Jeffreys, Esq.,
2 Thirlmere Gardens,
London
W6 7QR

Dear Sir,

In response to your inquiry, we have today asked our
Head Office to send to you a copy of our list of drawing-
books and materials, which we hope will interest you. I
think you will agree that all our products are very reason-
ably priced.

The items shown are but a few of the many types that we
stock. They will, however, give you a very fair idea of the
materials that we can offer. We carry larger stocks than
any other supplier in the area. All our materials are highly
recommended by the organizers of local Art Clubs throughout
the country.

We regret our inability to send you a more comprehensive
list: this is at present in the hands of our printer, and we
shall be pleased to forward a copy as soon as it is ready.

We hope that before placing your order for the coming
season you will give us an opportunity of sending you a
quotation for your requirements.

Yours faithfully,

D. J. Kingland
Sales Manager

Re-read the instructions on page 80 before typing the following exercises.

S P E C I F I C A T I O N of MATERIALS AND

WORKS for the construction of a MOTOR

GARAGE at 28 Sunnyfield Road, Nottingham,

for WILLIAM TORRINGTON, Esq., in

accordance with the drawing and the

particulars hereinafter specified.

JUNE, 19--

NOTE

The Contractor shall obtain and adopt for himself and upon his own responsibility all the information and particulars which may be necessary for the making of his tender and so indemnify Mr. William Torrington from any miscalculation in tendering or any other cause arising whatsoever during the execution and due fulfilment of this contract.

CHARACTER OF WORK

The whole of the work is to be completed in the best possible manner and in the style, character, and finish of first-class work.

MAKE GOOD

The Contractor shall at his own cost make good and reinstate all injury from wet, carelessness, or from any cause arising.

WORKS TO BE KEPT CLEAN

The surplus excavated material and rubbish to be removed from site as it accumulates, and as little inconvenience as possible caused to the owner during the execution of the work. The job must be left thoroughly tidy and neat each night.

PAYMENT

Payment will be made to the Contractor on completion in full providing that the work is to the entire satisfaction of Mr. William Torrington.

BRICK-LAYER

Break into existing disconnecting chambers and form connexions for 101·6 mm pipes from gullies and make good.

Provide and fix 101·6 mm pipe to fresh-air inlet at house and refix mica flap ventilator.

Provide and fix 101·6 mm pipe to form chamber for stopcock on water service.

All bricks to be well wetted before use. The whole of the brickwork to be in English bond in cement mortar—the facing brickwork in front of garage and also seen face as far as door leading to passage of house to be in best-quality red facing bricks. The remaining brickwork to be of ordinary yellow stock bricks of best quality built according to the drawing and to be set in true lines both horizontally and vertically with small regular joints all to be full bedded and cross jointed and flushed full of mortar.

Lay in walls a damp-proof course the full width of the wall composed of two courses of approved stout slates laid to mock joint in cement.

All external arches to doors at rear and side of garage and also window to be in red facing bricks.

Exercise 60

INDENTED style—First line of each paragraph indented.
Margin stops: Pica 12 and 72; Elite 20 and 80
Tab. stops: 17 or 26

Your ref: DR/BK   4th January, 19--
Our ref: AD/52

Messrs. R. J. Swayne & Son,
153 Colne Valley Road,
Nottingham,
NG2 4AL

Dear Sirs,

     In response to your application, we have pleasure in
enclosing a copy of our revised price list.

     From this you will see that owing to further economies
in manufacturing costs, made possible particularly by the
introduction of new machinery, we have been able to announce
a reduction in prices, which will take effect immediately.

     We believe that these reduced prices will serve to
encourage the use of the smaller sizes of our gas-filled
lamps, and we look forward to the pleasure of doing considerable business with you during the forthcoming season.

     Our representative, Mr. H. B. Yates, will be pleased
to visit you bringing with him samples of our full range of
lamps. Should you wish to contact him to arrange a convenient date and time, his telephone number is 061-970 207.

                    Yours faithfully,
               MORELAND & WESTERBY LIMITED

                                                   Manager

Enc.

Exercise 168

Your ref: BS/42   5th April, 19—
Our ref: PPW/BRL

Messrs. Beatty & Simpson,
Albion Works,
Cambridge CB5 9JJ

Dear Sirs,

In accordance with the request contained in your letter of 2nd April, our local representative has inspected your 3 x 2 x 3 boiler feed pump No. 82561.

To put this machine into first-class working order the following repairs and new parts will be required:—

(1) Steam cylinders require boring out and new rings supplied and fitted to existing pistons.

(2) New gunmetal liners are required for the water end, and existing gunmetal rings and pistons skimmed up to suit.

(3) The steam-chest faces require facing up, also the seats and valves in the water end; and two brass blocks are required.

Our price for supplying the above material and carrying out the repairs, including testing the pump would be

FORTY POUNDS
(£40)

The above price includes carriage to and from our works but we have not allowed for disconnecting or refixing.

We hope to be entrusted with the work and await your instructions.

Yours faithfully,

Manager

Type the following reports in double-line spacing.

Exercise 169

These units of electronic data processing systems are composed of electronic circuitry—valves, transistors, capacitors, etc.—and these are able to complete their operations at electronic speeds measured in millionths of a second. It is the electronic circuitry which is the secret of great speed in a computer. The arithmetical unit of the computer is able to carry out all the ordinary operations of addition, subtraction, multiplication and division, although in fact individual circuits can only add one digit at a time. Thus it carries out multiplication by continued addition and its almost incomprehensible speed enables it to

Exercise 169 (continued)

perform the calculation far more rapidly than any mechanical or electro-mechanical devices. The arithmetical and logical units of the digital computer of this kind employed in business use pulse techniques, and thus the language in which computers do their arithmetic is the Binary Code. Some computers, however, can be programmed in ordinary numbers and letters. The logical units of electronic data processing systems are sometimes referred to as the "decision making" sections.

Exercise 170

The Autoscale butter/margarine checkweigher was especially developed for butter and margarine packing lines for use with such equipment as the BDR Mark II. It is not a biscuit type checkweigher that has been adapted for a secondary function but is purpose designed.

All the points which are so important on a butter or margarine packing line have been taken into consideration. The equipment is waterproof and can be washed down. Setting up procedures and operation have been made so simple that any unskilled operator can operate it after five minutes' instruction. It is extremely accurate and the computer servo of the checkweigher will control the butter packing machine to its piston deviation plus 50% (so that if the difference in weight between pistons on a BDR is 4 grains, then the Autoscale will continuously keep the butter pats within a total tolerance of 6 grains). There are override facilities should any operator wish to increase or decrease weight regardless of the computer servo on the checkweigher. The reject mechanism is so designed that pats which are one or two grains under the target weight, but above the legal minimum weight, are not rejected, but only actual underweight pats are physically removed from the line.

The Autoscale checkweigher has no belt or other moving parts to require replacement or re-setting. The computer servo maintains a stable control despite variations in the line speed, occasional gross underweights, or overweights from a "wild" piston.

The Autoscale has not merely been designed so that it will cut down overweight and pay for itself: it will also make a profit for the butter packer.

The 400 series checkweigher is primarily designed for weighing to exceptionally high accuracies. We also manufacture the Autoscale D-100 for weighing cans and packs to 300 c.p.m., and the high speed Autoscale D-200 can checkweigher.

SEMI-BLOCKED style—Date and complimentary close as shown.
Margin stops: Pica 12 and 72; Elite 20 and 80
Tab. stops: 17 or 26

Notice the way in which the degrees are typed after the name of the
addressee. No space is left after the full stop.

ADV/25   5th August, 19--

Thomas Barclay, Esq., B.A., B.Sc.,
Regina House School,
OSWESTRY, Salop
SY11 3EE

Dear Sir,

Further to your enquiry for the costs involved in producing
a School Magazine, I would point out that, because of initial
preparation work involved, it will not be economic to consider
a quantity of less than 1,000.

On this basis, a magazine of 24 or even 32 pages of text,
printed on a light "book" paper, with an art paper inset of
4 pages to carry half-tone illustrations, all wire stitched
in a cover, size A5 (148 x 210 mm), could probably be produced
for approximately £150 - 15p each including block costs.

At this stage it is obviously impossible to submit a firm
quotation, but if the above is of interest I should be happy
to arrange for our representative to call to see you with
specimen of paper for cover and text, available types, etc.

When your needs are clarified and all the copy and photographs
are available, I shall be able to estimate final costs
accurately and submit rough layouts for suggested format.

I trust the above information will be useful and shall look
forward to co-operating with you in achieving an excellent
production.

                         Yours faithfully,
                         ASTRA PRINTERS LIMITED

                         G. Culliford

Enc.

TECHNICAL WORK

The shorthand-typist working in a business office is likely to be called upon to make copies of work of a technical or semi-technical nature. The following exercises give practice in typing this kind of work.

Pay particular attention to Exercise 171, and make yourself familiar with the layout of the specification shown there. Notice in particular the use of marginal headings, and use the margin-release lever when typing these. The body of a specification usually begins at about $2\frac{1}{2}$ in (63 mm) on the scale, and marginal headings at 1 in (25 mm). Double-line spacing is used for short specifications, and single-line spacing for long ones.

Exercise 165

Your ref: X/052   4th June, 19—
Our ref: PR/4/583

Messrs. R. Binns & Co.,
63 Parliament Road,
Bradford, Yorkshire BD5 7RJ

Dear Sirs,

The control gear we suggest is capable of operation by push button from your superintendent's office, which, we understand, is a quarter of a mile away from the centrifugal pump.

The gear would consist of our standard 40 h.p. starter motor, two electrically operated single-pole contractors, and one overload, with all the necessary resistances mounted behind the panel.

A double-pole hand-operated switch is provided in the main circuit, and this switch is mechanically interlocked with the containing case, so that the gear is inaccessible unless the switch is in the "off" position.

The contractors will operate successfully with a 20-per-cent voltage drop, so that a slight increase in the resistance of the control cable owing to bad weather will not affect them.

We should require to know the cross section and resistance of the control cable if you should decide on our apparatus.

Yours faithfully,

General Manager

Exercise 166

Your ref: RG/FTP   8th August, 19—
Messrs. Rupert Johnson & Sons,
Phoenix Works,
Leicester LE2 2BL

Dear Sirs,

We thank you for your letter of 6th August, and now submit particulars of magnet coils to your specification.

The bobbins are 76 mm long and 95·2 mm in diameter, made of brass tube with sheet brass flanges.

Micanite and Presspahn insulation is used throughout, permitting a winding space of 69·8 mm by 26 mm in which we wind 17,000 turns of No. 31 S.W.G. enamel-covered copper wire. One layer of paper is wrapped after every four layers of the wire to give the necessary cushion effect needed on account of the expansion caused by heat.

Allowing a current density of 160 amperes per square centimetre, these coils contain very nearly 1,797 ampere turns, which, we suggest, will suit your purpose.

In practice we find that these coils may be worked at a slightly higher current density without undue heating.

We shall be pleased to supply further particulars of our coils if you should require them.

Yours faithfully,
p.p. Benson Engineering Ltd.

Exercise 167

Our ref: D/PRY/AS   7th July, 19—
James Salcombe, Esq., F.C.I.S.,
The Cambridge Institute,
Bridge Road,
Aberdeen AB1 4EN

Dear Sir,

We have today made a careful examination of the defective rain-water pipe between your premises and No. 154 Bridge Road.

In our opinion the greater part of this rectangular pipe is cracked or broken. The lower lengths, however, are built into the retaining wall of the area and are not accessible.

The size $4\frac{1}{8}''$ by $4\frac{1}{8}''$ is now obsolete, and we suggest that a pipe 101 mm by 101 mm should be substituted. It would perhaps be worth while considering a 101 mm circular-pattern rain-water pipe, as the difference in the cost of a 1·83 m length of ordinary 101 mm circular pipe and a 101 mm by 101 mm rectangular pipe is no less than 55p.

Instead of the lower lengths of this pipe being put into the wall as at present, we think it would be advisable to fix offsets and carry the pipe down into the area.

We should be glad to arrange for our Mr. Peterson to call upon you to discuss this matter.

Yours faithfully,

P. R. Young

Exercise 62

24th July, 19--

Your ref: BRK/FL
Our ref: DE/LK

Messrs. Jules Picard & Fils,
Hairdressers,
4416 Regent Street,
London
W1R 5PL

Dear Sirs,

May we, please, have your cheque in payment of
... the enclosed account?

It is doubtless quite unnecessary for us to do
more than point out that this account is now
overdue, because we are sure that you have no
more desire to inconvenience us than we have
to write to you for money. Our prices and
other arrangements are fixed on the basis of
monthly settlements and net terms, so that
punctual payments are essential.

Perhaps you will be good enough to send with
your cheque your inquiries for any soaps and
perfumes you may be requiring shortly.

... We have pleasure in enclosing a copy of our
latest price-list which includes a number of
our new products that we now have in stock.

Yours faithfully,
BENSON, DAY & CO. LTD.

D. Evans
Credit Controller

Set out the following as an advertisement, leaving 3 in (76 mm) between the first and second lines for an illustration of the garage.

EXTRA! EXTRA! WAVELING DOUBLE GARAGE!

The new "Wideway" concrete garage is <u>extra</u> wide.

Two door openings 2·28 x 1·9 m

Internal width 4·85 m

    "   height 2·21 m

Lengths: a variety to suit all purposes

Roof: specially designed asbestos

Red/ Materials: Western / Cedar or Deal doors

            x x x x x

Many other models – single garages, double garages, multiple garages – to suit every car and every site

           detailed and

Write for our / fully illustrated brochure to:-

WALTER WAVELING LIMITED

13 Ebury Road, Bournemouth, BH1 1RN

Avenue/ 97 College/Road, Manchester, M23 0LB

134 Old Bank Street, London, W1N 0BD

Exercise 63

Remember that nothing should appear with the post code in the last
line of the address.

Your ref: JB/IK   12th March, 19--
Our ref: DSK/LT

The Manager,
The Central Domestic Stores,
58 Percival Road,
Shrewsbury
SY3 0LH

Dear Sir,

We thank you for your letter of 10th March, concerning
the price charged to you for the lubricating oil that we
recently supplied.

We regret to say that, owing to the heavy freight and
other charges now ruling, we have been compelled to make an
increase in our prices.

You will no doubt remember that at one time freight
represented approximately only 1p per litre on the cost of
the oil: as a result of recent increases it now represents
no less than $7\frac{1}{2}$p per litre. With these figures in mind, we
feel sure you will agree that our increased price is a very
moderate one.

Since the last delivery we made to you, we have been
compelled to make a further increase of $1\frac{1}{2}$p per litre for
the "A" quality, which we have been in the habit of supplying to you.

We hope that before long there will be a drop in freight
charges, which will enable us to reduce our prices to their
normal level.

Yours faithfully,

Manager

Exercise 162

Set out the following in two columns, listing the equipment alphabetically under sections. These sections should be: General Classroom Equipment; Office and Library Furniture and Equipment; Scientific Apparatus and Equipment; and Building Department Furniture and Equipment.

MAIN SUPPLIERS OF FURNITURE AND EQUIPMENT

Educational Supply Association, Watford	Classroom desks and chairs
The Art Metal Co. Ltd., London	Laboratory benches
Kingfisher Ltd., London	Typewriter chairs
Dowdeswells Ltd., Guildford	Office furniture
F. A. Riches & Son Ltd., Little Britain, London	Typewriters and office machinery
Papworth Industries, Cambridge	Classroom cupboards
Wilson & Garden Ltd., Glasgow	"Unique" revolving blackboards
Drawing Equipment Production Ltd., York	Drawing boards and Tee squares
W. Birch Ltd., High Wycombe	Laboratory stools
Libraco Ltd., London	Library furniture
Wadkins Ltd., Leicester	Woodworking machines
The Clipper Manufacturing Co. Ltd., Leicester	Brick cutting machine
Pioneer Mixers Ltd., Monkseaton	Roller pan mill brickwork shop
F. J. Edwards Ltd., London	Machine tools
S. Denison & Son Ltd., Leeds	Testing machines for concrete
W. & T. Avery Ltd., London	Balances and test machines, building science laboratory
J. W. Towers & Co. Ltd., Widnes	Balances, building science laboratory
Griffin & Tatlock, London	Scientific equipment
Gallenkamp, London	Scientific apparatus
British Drug Houses Ltd., Poole	Chemicals
Barker Peacham Ltd., Richmond	Library books
A. J. Allen (High Wycombe) Ltd., Aylesbury	Boardroom chairs
Phillip Harris Ltd., Birmingham	Biological apparatus
T. Gerrard & Co. Ltd., London	Biological supplies
Educational & Scientific Plastics Ltd., Croydon	Scientific models
Hawksley & Sons Ltd., London	Scientific instruments
The British Oxygen Co. Ltd., Wembley	Oxygen and acetylene welding plant

Exercise 163

Use A4 paper turned sideways. Centre a ruled rectangle measuring 22·0 × 5·7 cm and divide this, by ruling, into five smaller rectangles each measuring 4·3 × 5·7 cm. In the rectangles, type alphabetically the names given below (keeping to the same grouping), centring them both vertically and horizontally.

Pycamisan	Methotrexate	Mebryl	Aventyl	Flagyl
Imuran	Serensil	Librium	Lingraine	Decadron
Atromid-S	Dexedrine	Orbenin	Oblivon	Camoprima
Enavid-E	Chloromycetin	Lederkyn	Mysoline	Secrodyl

Margin stops: Pica 12 and 72; Elite 20 and 80

Remember that no punctuation is used in the post code in the last line of the address.

10th June, 19--

DEM/55

The Secretary,
Messrs. Abingdon & Panzetta,
532 Broad Street,
London
W4 5QR

Dear Sir,

We shall be pleased to have the opportunity of placing before you
particulars of our special maintenance contracts for electric-
lighting installations and motors.

The question of efficient maintenance is of great importance to
all users of electricity as it keeps the installation in thorough
repair, thus minimizing the risk of breakdown and subsequent
dislocation of work.

We enclose details of a recent maintenance programme carried through
by our engineers which clearly shows the subsequent advantages of
our service to this client. You will notice in the comparative table
of breakdowns and losses in production, that since a regular
maintenance contract was signed with this organization the volume of
production has increased.

Will you let us know when it would be convenient for our representative
to call and discuss the matter, as we are sure that you will find that
the arrangements we offer will show considerable advantages.

Yours faithfully,

R. Jones
Sales Manager

Enc.

Exercise 161

Set out the statement below in two columns on A4 paper, so that the receipts side is alongside the payments side. Fold the paper in half (across the longer sides) before inserting it into the machine.

Summary of Liquidator's Accounts

1st January to 31st May 19..

RECEIPTS

£

To Balance	80213.94
" Receipts, viz -	
Interest on Investments	1936.65
Interest on Deposit	106.52
General Average refunds & recoveries	2308.37
" Foreign Liquidator :-	
Amt. remitted under Canadian surplus agreement	65587.02
" Book debts - Good	511.14
	150663.64
Less refund of amount overpaid	200.00
	£ 150463.64

PAYMENTS £

By Board of Trade and Court Fees	22.38
" Other Law costs	40.00
" Other charges (rent, wages, travelling etc.	745.50
" Incidental outlay	26.68
Total cost and charges	834.56
Unsecured creditors :-	
First and 2nd dividend of 20p in the £ on £4405.56	881.11
Third dividend of 15p in the £ on £702454.88	105368.23
First Second & third dividend of 35p in the £ on £3346.28	1171.20
Balance	42208.54
	£ 150463.64

77

Abbreviations

Exercises 65–8 contain lists of some abbreviations in use in business offices. You should be familiar with these, as you will find that many of them occur frequently in business correspondence. It is becoming increasingly prevalent for abbreviations to be typed without stops (particularly if the last letter of the abbreviation is the last letter of the word). However, in the following lists, the stops are at present retained. Type each exercise once, underscoring words in italics.

Margin stops: Pica 12 and 72; Elite 20 and 80
Tab stops: 41 or 49

Exercise 65

abs.	absolute(ly), abstract
a/c or acct.	account
A.D.	*Anno Domini* (in the year of our Lord)
ad. or advt.	advertisement
ad lib.	*ad libitum* (at pleasure)
ad val. or a/v	*ad valorem* (according to value)
afft.	affidavit
agt.	agent
a.m.	*ante meridiem* (before noon)
amt.	amount
anon.	anonymous
appro.	approval
a/r	all risks
arr.	arrange(d) arrive(d)
A/S	account sales
asst.	assistant
av.	average
B.A.	Bachelor of Arts
B.Com.	Bachelor of Commerce
b.e.	bill of exchange
b.f.	brought forward
B/L	bill of lading
bldg.	building
bro(s).	brother(s)
b.s.	balance sheet, bill of sale
B.Sc.	Bachelor of Science
C.	centigrade, century
c.	cent, centime, cubic, copy
c.	*circa* (about)
cap.	capital letter
cat.	catalogue
cc.	copies circulated to
c.d. or cum div.	with dividend
c.f.	carried forward
cf. or cp.	compare
ch.	chapter
c.i.f.	cost, insurance, freight

Exercise 66

cm.	centimetre
c.n.	credit note, consignment note
Co.	Company, County
c/o	care of
C.O.D.	cash on delivery
com.	commission
cr.	credit, creditor
cwt.	hundredweight
d.a.	days after acceptance, Deposit Account
deb.	debenture
decd.	deceased
dft.	draft
dis.	discount
div.	divide, dividend
d.n.	debit note
doll. or d.	dollar(s)
dr.	doctor, debtor, drawer
D.Sc.	Doctor of Science
E. & O.E.	errors and omissions excepted
E.E.	errors excepted
E.F.T.A.	European Free Trade Association
e.g.	*exempli gratia* (for example)
enc(s).	enclosure(s)
eq.	equal
etc.	*et cetera* (and so on)
et. seq.	*et sequens* (and the following)
ex.	examined, example, exchange
ex div. or x.d.	without dividend
ex int. or x.i.	without interest
F.	Fahrenheit
fcp.	foolscap
f.o.b.	free on board
ft.	foot, feet
g.	gramme
gal.	gallon(s)
G.L.C.	Greater London Council

Exercise 160

Type the Summary of Assets and Liabilities on A5 paper, landscape (with the longest dimension at the top). Calculate the horizontal and vertical centring with care (*see page* 54). Check all the figures before removing the typescript from the machine.

The total items should be centred between the ruled lines above and below. To obtain this effect type the line above the total; turn the paper up twice before typing the total; then turn the paper up once only before typing the double line below the total. Remember that the totals should appear level at the foot of the summary.

Insert the name of the company, Ross and Mye Limited, above the heading. Type below the headings 'as at 30 September 1971.'

Summary of Assets and Liabilities

Liabilities	£	Assets	£
Sundry Creditors	23,598.35	Cash in hand	29.13
Bank Loan	6,897.07	Petty Cash in hand	2.66
W. Smith : Loan	589.12	Stock at Cost	9,852.43
H. Jones : 9 months' Rent to 29th Sept. last	250.00	Fixtures and Fittings	529.36
Rates : 6 months to 31st March last	132.15	Office Furniture	462.80
		Sundry Debtors	5,289.17
	£31,466.69	Freehold Property	8,589.14
			£29,038.61

Bills Receivable £4,283.92

Exercise 67

G.M.T.	Greenwich Mean Time
hon.	honorary, honourable
H.M.S.	Her Majesty's Service, Her Majesty's Ship
h.p.	hire purchase, horse power
hr(s).	hour(s)
ib. or ibid.	*ibidem* (in the same place)
id.	*idem* (the same)
i.e.	*id est* (that is)
in.	inch, inches
ital.	italic (sloping) print
Junr., Jr.	Junior
kg. or kilo	kilogramme
kil., kilom. or km.	kilometre(s)
kw.	kilowatt
lat.	latitude
lb.	pound(s)
L/C	letter of credit
l.c.	lower case
LL.B.	Bachelor of Laws
LL.D.	Doctor of Laws
long.	longitude
m.	metre(s), million, month
M.A.	Master of Arts
M.B.	Bachelor of Medicine
M.D.	Doctor of Medicine
memo	memorandum
mfg.	manufacturing
misc.	miscellaneous
MM.	*Messieurs*
mm.	millimetre
M.O.	money order
M.P.	Member of Parliament
m.p.g.	miles per gallon
m.p.h.	miles per hour
MS(S).	manuscript(s)
mth.	month
n/a	no account
N.A.T.O.	North Atlantic Treaty Organization
N.B.	*nota bene* (note well)
nem. con.	*nemine contradicente* (no-one contradicting)
N.P.	new paragraph
nr.	near
non seq.	*non sequitur* (it does not follow)
no(s).	number(s)
O/D	on demand, overdraft
O.E.C.D.	Organisation for Economic Co-operation and Development
O.H.M.S.	On Her Majesty's Service
o/s	out of stock, outstanding
oz.	ounce(s)

Exercise 68

p., pp.	page, pages
p.a.	per annum
par. or para.	paragraph
P.A.Y.E.	pay as you earn
P.C.	Privy Council(lor)
p.c.	per cent, postcard
p/c	petty cash, prices current
pd.	paid
per pro. or p.p.	*per procurationem* (on behalf of)
P/L	profit and loss
p.m.	*post meridiem* (after noon)
P.O.	post office, postal order
pro tem.	*pro tempore* (for the time being)
P.S.	*postscriptum* (postscript)
pt.	part, payment, pint
P.T.O.	Please turn over
qr.	quarter
qt.	quart
q.v.	*quod vide* (which see)
R/D	Refer to drawer
rec.	receipt, record
ref.	referred, reference
reg.	register, regular
rm.	ream
rep.	report, representative
retd.	returned
R.P.	reply paid
R.S.V.P.	répondez s'il vous plaît (please reply)
S.S. or S/S	steamship
sgd.	signed
stg.	sterling
temp.	temperature, temporary
trs.	transpose
transf.	transferred
T.U.C.	Trades Union Congress
u.c.	upper case
U.N.O.	United Nations Organization
U.N.E.S.C.O.	United Nations Educational, Scientific and Cultural Organization
U.N.R.R.A.	United Nations Relief Rehabilitation Administration
v.	*versus* (against)
vide	*vide* (see)
vs.	against, *versus*
w.	with
W.H.O.	World Health Organization
wt.	weight
yd.	yard(s)

SHRINES OF FRANCE

13 days - no night travel - £58.25

ABRIDGED ITINERARY

← → Day 1 London - Paris

Depart London, Victoria 0630. 0900 Newhaven - Dieppe Service.)

run on

⌐ Luxury coach meets you upon arrival at Dieppe, proceed to Paris.

Hôtel Terminus Nord, 12 bd de Denain PARIS — DINNER & OVERNIGHT

Day 2 Paris - Bourges

Leave Paris at 1000 for →

where /

Chartres for / lunch will be served. At least one hour is allowed for a visit to the Cathedral.

SALBRIS

Over the lovely River Loire /

Continue drive via Orléans, with its beautiful châteaux, / to Bourges via Vierzon, arriving Salbris for tea-break.

Hôtel du Parc

BOURGES — DINNER & OVERNIGHT

Evening at leisure.

LEISURE

~~Day 3 Bourges~~

75

Typing Sums of Money

Leave no space between the amount and p for pence. No full stop should be used after the p unless it ends a sentence. If the £ sign is used do NOT type the pence abbreviation as well; always type two digits after the decimal point (plus ½ for halfpenny where required).

Study the following examples:—

1. Pence only: 97p or £0·97
2. Pence and halfpennies: 98½p or £0·98½
3. Halfpenny only: ½p or £0·00½
4. Pounds and pence: £29·60

Margin stops: Pica 15 and 70; Elite 24 and 79

Type the exercises on this page in single-line spacing, with double-line spacing between paragraphs.

Exercise 69

Your ref: 2146/J   11th March, 19—
Our ref: DRC/AJ

Messrs. Simpson, Carr & Co.,
83 Swadford Street,
Cardiff CF6 6AU

Dear Sirs,

We thank you for your letter of 10th March, regarding the purchase of the S.S. "Speedway."

It is assumed that you require a quotation on an "All risks" basis, i.e. Institute Time Clauses, and the best rate we have been able to secure on her is £16·60 per cent, subject to Institute Warranties, and on a valuation of twenty-eight thousand pounds (£28,000).

We presume you will also wish to cover the full amount of 10 per cent on Disbursements and 15 per cent on Freight and we feel sure we should be able to cover these at £3 per cent and £4·50 per cent respectively.

We look forward to hearing further from you.
      Yours faithfully,

Exercise 71

BRY/flc   30th November, 19—

Mrs. J. Walters,
12 Green Lanes,
Portsmouth, Hampshire Po7 5BA

Dear Mrs. Walters,

Thank you for your letter of 28th November in which you ask for Swiss currency for your forthcoming visit to Switzerland.

Foreign currency cannot be issued without the production of an up-to-date passport. If you will either bring in or send your current passport to us, and let us know the sum you require, bearing in mind the present Government restrictions on the issue of foreign currency, we shall be glad to meet your requirements.
      Yours sincerely,
      B. R. Young

Manager

Exercise 70

      4th July, 19—
B. T. Smith, Esq.,
Williamson & Prentice Ltd.,
247 Oppenheim Street,
Luton,
Bedfordshire LU1 3HJ

Dear Sir,

We thank you for your inquiry of 3rd July and have pleasure in enclosing five booklets giving full details, including the revised prices, of our latest models of spirit and rotary duplicators.

We feel that a visit to our Showrooms would enable you to find out which duplicator best meets your needs. Our Manager will be most pleased to give you a demonstration whenever it is convenient for you to call there. Alternatively, our Representative for your area could visit you at your office to give you further information.

Should you be interested in any model not covered by the booklets, please let us know.
      Yours faithfully,

Encs. (5)

Exercise 72

BS/DD   5th June, 19—

W. J. Parker, Esq.,
c/o 28 Sunnyville Road,
London N9 9ST

Dear Sir,

We thank you for your order No. 71462 of 4th June, and have to inform you that we are expecting delivery of this size and fitting of boot from our factory not later than the end of next week.

We shall send a pair to you immediately they arrive.

We are glad to know that the two pairs previously supplied have given you satisfaction, as we recognize that a satisfied customer is our best advertisement.

We enclose the receipt of payment for your previous purchases, as requested.
      Yours faithfully,

Enc.

Type the following two exercises to achieve an attractive display.

Exercise 158

Contents

Preface

Part I

1x ~~the~~ ↑

Part II

Type the following exercises on this page in single-line spacing, with double-line spacing between paragraphs. Insert the date when this is not given. Note the "open punctuation" style: this is frequently used.

Margin stops: Pica 15 and 70; Elite 24 and 79

Exercise 73

Your ref BRO/4
Our ref BEK/LM

The Secretary
The Santos Institute
Newcastle-upon-Tyne NE1 4EB

Dear Sir

We thank you for your order for 150 kg of washing compound, which is receiving our immediate attention.

We note your request for fine bags, which we presume is to prevent any trouble with leakage. We have therefore executed your order by sending you our washing compound in outer bags containing small brown-paper packets of compound, and three tins, to make up the weight to 150 kg. You will find these bags far more economical in use than the sacks, as there will be no leakage whatever, and they are specially suitable for your particular use. You will, of course, appreciate that the packings sent to you cost more than the 50 kg bags, but, as we have done this on our own responsibility, we are invoicing you at bulk rate, £2·12 per 50 kg.

Yours faithfully

Exercise 74

ADU/48

Messrs Knott Brothers
Lechdale Works
Newport Mon NP6 4SA

Dear Sirs

Our district agent informs us that you have not yet received a quotation for the annual premium payable for placing your electric-light and bell installation completely in our charge.

We have requested our agent not to call upon you, as this is often inconvenient. As, however, we do not wish you to miss this opportunity of realizing the great value and convenience to you of our complete service, we are sending you herewith a card which you have only to return to us and you will receive a quotation without delay and quite without obligation.

The reverse side of this card is a specimen of our special monthly inspection card, as used by our staff in the service of our clients.

Post this card back to us now.

Yours faithfully

Enc

Exercise 75

The Secretary
The Eastern Packing & Export Co Ltd
246 Phoenix Wharf
London E6 4DA

Dear Sir

May we have the pleasure of sending you a quotation for the maintenance or repair of any of your lifts, cranes, or other machinery?

Our works are well equipped with all classes of lathes, drilling, shaping, and planing machines, including one of the longest screw-cutting lathes in London.

We shall be pleased to give you a price for the maintenance of your machines, and we wish to point out that our system differs considerably from most others in that our quotations include all materials used, such as motor brushes, oil, packing, leathers, etc., thus saving you unnecessary correspondence and worry.

Our representative will be pleased to call upon you at any time to suit your convenience and give whatever information you may require.

Yours faithfully

Exercise 76

Your ref FL/456
Our ref DL/BD

The Manager
Donaldson Advertising Agency
10 Dorchester Road
Birmingham B17 OSW

Dear Sir

We thank you for your letter of 6th June and have pleasure in giving the following revised estimate for reprinting in black, binding and wrapping 1,000 copies of the booklet entitled "A History of Tea-drinking in England."

For supplying 1,000 crown A4 copies from standing type and blocks; folding 1 × 16 and 1 × 8 page sections; wire-stitched; cut flush; limp paper wrapper, two-colour printed; for the sum of £80.

We trust that this revised estimate will be acceptable to you, and look forward to hearing from you in the course of the next few days.

Yours faithfully

Type the following advertisement and insert a post code in the address.

ADVERTISING - AGENCY MANAGEMENT

Corbet & Manning Ltd.

have 2 outstanding opportunities to offer to experienced agency men.

As Manager of their office in Ecuador. This is a position with a tremendous future in a rapidly expanding area for a man who wants new horizons. This man will have -

1. Agency management experience.
2. Exp. of a Latin market. 3. Fluent Spanish-

A senior management position with their affiliated Co. in Stuttgart. Fluent German and some experience of the European market essential.

Candidates for both appls. shd. be between 30 and 40 and now earning not less than £3,500. Applications with full details should be addressed to -

Staff Director, C & M Ltd., Manson House Elton Place, London, W.1.

Typist: write out

(All applications will be treated in ~~the~~ strictest confidence.)

73

Continuation Sheets

When a letter occupies more than one page, the second and subsequent pages are described as continuation sheets. These sheets are of the same size and quality as the first sheet used but do not have a printed letter heading. About 1 in (25 mm) from the top of the continuation sheet the name of the addressee is typed at the left-hand margin, the number of the page is centred to the writing line e.g. -2-, and the date is typed so that it ends level with the right-hand margin. The letter is then continued on the third single space below the name. If the name of the addressee is very long the page number may be typed above the line for the name and date.

When a continuation sheet is required, the letter must be arranged so that at least three or four lines are typed on the second page. It is also preferable to leave at least two lines of a paragraph at the bottom of the first page. Be careful not to divide words, proper nouns, sums of money or sets of figures, at the bottom of the page. In the fully-blocked style the page number is typed at the left-hand margin, followed by the date and addressee's name, double-line spaced.

Exercise 77

Margin stops: Pica 15 and 70; Elite 24 and 79

Ref.   Pub/BSA   5th April, 19--

P. R. Locksley, Esq.,
41 Quentin Street,
Brighton, Sussex,
BN1 3WA

Dear Sir,

Towards the end of February an announcement was made informing the public of the proposed formation of a club for members of the British Stage Association. As a result, many inquiries have been received about the possibility of members of the general public supporting this venture.

The provisional Committee set up to launch the club feel that many people would be only too willing to support by voluntary donations a club for members of the theatrical profession – a profession which in the past has always shown its willingness to help any appeal made by other organizations and charities, and will unhesitatingly continue to do so. But on this rare occasion we are seeking support from the general public for ourselves.

This club will be of great importance to all and will, it is hoped, benefit especially the younger members who are unable to afford the more expensive clubs open to members of the profession. A most important need, which it is felt the club will fulfil, is to provide a place of relaxation for use between rehearsals and as a port of call to take the place of the weary hours spent in railway waiting-rooms when members are in transit through London – a building which will provide the usual social amenities of a club, and will, of course, include the provision of meals at reasonable cost. It is also hoped that in due course it will be possible to provide residential accommodation so that artistes travelling to London on business will be able to obtain comfortable rooms at a reasonable cost.

The club must be run as a financially self-supporting concern, but first several thousand pounds must be found to

Exercise 156

Type this extract from Professor Morgan's book in double-line spacing.

Many people think of economics as an abstract and theoretical study; in fact, it has grown up, like most other branches of human knowledge, from the efforts of a large number of men and women to grapple with some very practical problems. Our first efforts in any new field are ~~usually~~ scattered and feeble, based on scanty observations and imperfect reasoning: then more abundant and accurate information is gathered, and the technique of analysis is refined; the range of problems studied is extended, and it becomes apparent that relation-ships observed in one situation hold good in others; and so we have the emergence of scientific "laws." Finally students become conscious of a group of situations, bound together by the operations of such "laws" and set apart, with suitable modifications from other types of situation to which these laws do not apply.

From "A First Approach to Economics," by E. Victor Morgan

72

P. R. Locksley, Esq.   -2-   5th April, 19--

cover the capital expenses of starting such a venture. To
this end, therefore, an Equipment Fund has been opened.
Donations to this Fund should be sent to John Field, Hon.
Secretary, British Stage Association Club Ltd., 2 Lark Street,
London W1Y 3RL.

Arrangements have been made to hold a Midnight Gala
Show on the 30th September when many well-known members of
the theatrical profession have agreed to donate their services free and the Managers of the Apollo Theatre have kindly
undertaken to grant us the use of the theatre at a nominal
rent. Further details of this function will be sent to you
shortly and I hope you will be able to support this venture.
Tickets will be available at £5.50, £3.50 and £1.25 each.

Yours faithfully,

Margin stops: Pica 20 and 64; Elite 30 and 74

Line-space lever for single-line spacing. Leave 3 in (76 mm) at the top of the paper
before typing the reference.

Exercise 78

Your ref AYB/Inq/54
Our ref GRD/EL

Messrs Packinson Laive & Sons
42 Benton Street
London E8 3SG

Dear Sirs

Thank you for your letter of 6th May, asking our opinion of the prospects of introducing into this country a good make of fountain pen.

From a very close estimate we have formed from first-hand information, we believe that the value of fountain pens imported into South America is approximately £10,000 per annum. About 65 per cent of the sales are in Rio and Sao Paulo.

The majority come from the United States, and one American manufacturer, having established his name and trade-mark, has a local representative. Two other American fountain pens are sold in small quantities by salesmen who make occasional visits to Brazil. Recently one German pen has been introduced, but it does not offer much competition.

There is no doubt that for selling fountain pens it is advantageous to have a live local representative handling other non-conflicting lines. We are prepared to represent you here for your product on the terms indicated in your letter, but we suggest that an additional five-per-cent discount should be allowed to us on the under-

standing that we pay for consignments by cash against documents in London.

If these terms are agreeable to you, will you please forward immediately a trial consignment, in accordance with the particulars on the order form which we now enclose.

Yours faithfully
pp David Anson Ltd
G R Dobson
Enc

Exercise 79

Your ref: Adv./DG
Our ref: PR/OYB4

Messrs. Higgins and Bell,
16 Wallace Place,
London N1 2PG

Dear Sirs,

Thank you for the leaflets which you sent us yesterday. I should be glad if you would kindly let us have a further quantity, say two thousand, within a week. I wonder whether these could be printed in a different colour from the original blue which, while quite satisfactory, is a little less striking than the sample which you sent in orange. We have used the blue copies for our preliminary distribution but, if it would involve no additional cost, we should like a further thousand in orange and the second thousand in a vivid green. As you know, these are the colours of our organization, and we should like to use them

Exercise 155

Type the following letter taking one carbon copy and addressing an envelope. Insert a post code.

29 Park Road,
Manchester M10 7JH

9 January, 19--

W. Snail, Esq.,
Stanley Court,
Russell Rd, London, E.C.1.

Dear Sir,

I think there is much to be said for the views you expressed in your letter of 4 January. Variations in page sizes are not only expensive but also exceptionally inconvenient. The additional expense involved in having special blocks and drawings made for certain papers is quite a considerable item in proportion to the total cost of buying and filling the space in these papers. It seems absurd that one should have to spend possibly £4 or £5 on a revised drawing & new original half-tone block to occupy space which itself costs no more than that amt. of money. Standardization of page size must sooner or later come. Individual papers will, in adopting a standard page size, have their particular difficulties to surmount. Time, however, will not lessen these difficulties but will rather tend to accentuate them. Any objections which may be raised now, will be still more cogent in five or ten years' time. Every month & every year of further delay in this vital matter means additional TROUBLE and expense when the change is finally made.

Yours faithfully,

P.S. I am returning the special report.

71

if possible. Perhaps you would let me know if this change of colour could be managed and whether it would make any difference to the final cost.

I should also like to discuss the question of tickets. We propose making an issue of 250 free seats and we suggest that the remainder of the seats should be priced at 25p. I shall leave the wording of the ticket to you, although I should naturally like the name of our organization to be prominently displayed. Apart from this, I shall be happy to leave the matter in your hands.

Finally, may I say how much we appreciate your generosity in handling this printing work for us at cost price. It will make a big difference to our calculations, and we naturally wish to keep expenses low so that our donation to charity may be as substantial as possible. Thank you again for all your help in this matter.

Yours faithfully,
Branch President

Carbon Copying

It is necessary to retain at least one copy of every letter dispatched from a business house. The most common method of doing this is to use sheets of carbon paper. The sheets of paper on which copies are made are usually thinner than the top sheet, and they are known as "flimsies." To make a carbon copy, place your top sheet face downwards on your desk. On top of it, place a sheet of carbon paper, glossy side upwards and then place on it the flimsy, face downwards. Adjust the edges of the sheets of paper, and insert them into the machine, holding the top sheet away from you.

An alternative method is to insert the top sheet and flimsies into the typewriter about half an inch. Then arrange the carbon paper between the sheets of typewriting paper, glossy side facing forward. Now complete the turning of the set of papers into the machine.

If it is necessary to erase remember to move the carriage to the side, insert a piece of paper or card between the carbon and the copy, and erase gently.

Take a carbon copy of each of the following exercises. Line-space lever for single-line spacing.

Margin stops: Pica 15 and 70; Elite 24 and 79

Exercise 80

ADV/92   10th April, 19—

The Manager,
Advertising Dept.,
The Unique Pen & Pencil Co.,
Leicester LE4 7JR

Dear Sir,

A good "form letter" is the cheapest, most effective and most productive means of direct publicity that can be employed in nearly every form of "selling" or propaganda.

Within our organization we have the experience, the ability and the equipment to plan, write, illustrate, print and post any form of commercial literature. We can meet your individual requirements and help to increase the sale of your goods.

Quite recently we made ours a complete postal publicity service by organizing a Plan and Copy Department and placing it under the general direction of a postal publicity expert of international reputation. Years of practical and successful work in the United States and Canada as well as in this country have taught him the essentials of success in the economical direct-by-post method of sales promotion.

We should be glad to be of service to you.

Yours faithfully,

Exercise 81

JBS/24   6th August, 19—

W. Benskin, Esq., M.D., M.R.C.S.,
Europa House,
Clacton, Essex CL2 8PZ

Dear Sir,

I hope you will be pleased with the enclosed copy of the Report for the year ended 30th June last, which was presented at the Annual Meeting of the Society, held today.

The transactions of this, the first year of our new quinquennium, hold out great promise for the future. In this connexion you will be pleased to notice that a profit of £250,000 has been made on securities realized, and that there has been a very marked appreciation in the value of the Stock Exchange and other securities.

The net rate of interest earned was £6·25 per cent. This rate is £2·00 per cent more than the rate assumed in our Valuation, and is the highest ever earned in the 98 years the Society has been in existence. As the Life Assurance Fund amounts to £10,000,000 this margin of interest has yielded over £200,000 profit during the year.

All these features lead me to repeat what I advised a year ago, that it is better to effect With-profit or Prime-cost Policies and become partners in our success.

Enc.   Yours faithfully,

Before typing the following exercises, re-read Exercise 153. Remember that a single line under a word means that the word should be underscored when typing (a printer would italicize it); a double line under a word means that it should be typed in capitals; three lines under a word indicates spaced capitals. Notice that three full stops, sometimes spaced as at the end of Exercise 154, are used to indicate that an extract is unfinished. Omissions are known as ellipsis, and the typist also uses three full stops for the omissions of groups of words at the beginning and in the middle of a sentence. When such an omission comes at the end of a sentence the ordinary full stop follows the three full stops, as in the following example:—

```
... and many motorists will be preparing for the holiday

ordeal, wondering where to pack all the luggage and ...

cooped up with restless children.  A roof rack is the

answer to most ....
```

Exercise 154

```
              In all countries, however, men seem at last to
eq; #    have been determined | by various reasons to give
    #    the preference for this employment, to metals
O/Gp/    above every other commodity, metals cannot be
trs/     (only) kept with as little loss as any other
ey/      commodity, scarce anything being less perishable
         than they are, but they can likewise, without
# l.c./  any loss, be divided into any number of parts, as
  -/     by fusion those parts can easily be reunited; a
  i/     quality which no other equally durable commodties
  q/     possess, and which more than any other quality
 stet    renders them fit to be the instruments of commerce
N.P. l.c/ l.c/ and circulation. [The men who wanted to buy salt
         for example, and had nothing but cattle to give in
  ,/     exchange ...
```

Take a carbon copy of each of the following exercises.

Margin stops: Pica 12 and 72; Elite 22 and 82

Line-space lever for single-line spacing

Exercise 82

AB/CL   6th March, 19—

Douglas Fenton, Esq., J.P.,
8 Oaklands,
Paignton TQ4 6HX

Dear Sir,

We thank you for your inquiry of 5th March, regarding the discount allowed on orders for our "Warewhel" Special Furnishings.

On orders received from you some years ago we allowed you a special discount of five per cent. We regret, however, that in consequence of the prevailing conditions and the high cost of production, we have been compelled to compile our present catalogue on a strictly net cash basis.

In these circumstances we are sorry that we are unable to extend to you the same concession as formerly, but, in view of our past business relationships, we shall be pleased to allow you a discount of five per cent on all individual orders of £20 in value or over.

You may be assured that we shall offer you the benefit of any future relief in production costs.

Yours faithfully,

Exercise 83

LD/128   4th December, 19—

G. S. Roberts, Esq.,
15 Broad Street,
Newton Abbot TQ13 8LS

Dear Sir,

Thank you for your letter of 2nd December, in which you make inquiries about the possibility of securing an overdraft on your current account at this Branch.

I am sure you will appreciate that, in the present economic state of the country, it is possible to grant credit facilities of this nature only under very special circumstances; and from the information given in your letter I think it is unlikely that your case can be considered to fall into this category. If, however, you would care to call to see me, we could discuss the matter in more detail. It would be necessary for me to have a copy of your last audited accounts; and satisfactory security would have to be produced or, failing that, you would need to nominate guarantors acceptable to the Bank.

Yours faithfully,
Manager

Exercise 84

DBC/RA   10th March, 19—

The Manager,
The Universal Stores Ltd.,
83 Stone Street,
London WC1E 7DE

Dear Sir,

Thank you for your letter of 9th March, regarding likely shops for your business.

One that I think would suit you (the lease of which I have for disposal) is in the High Street, Deptford.

The shop has a frontage of 5·5 m and a depth of 17·7 m, is elaborately built, and is 4·6 m in height. There is a basement, about 5·5 m by 7·3 m deep, which is convenient for stores and very dry.

There are no shops running the same class of business as yours near the site, and it would seem to me to be an excellent position for you.

The rent would be £600 per annum for a lease of 21 years. I may mention that the premises are assessed at £280 per annum, and that the rates are at present 60p in the £.

I can arrange for you to view the premises at your convenience.

Yours faithfully,

Exercise 85

Your ref: BK/LM
Our ref: SRBL/561

Messrs. Pearson & Whiteley,
39 Grove Road,
BOLTON, Lancashire BL1 3PG

Dear Sirs,

We thank you for your inquiry of 7th April for 1,000 reams A4 and 500 reams A5 Bond and Bank paper. Our price list is enclosed.

We have pleasure in sending samples of "A" Quality and "B" Quality. Delivery can be guaranteed within 10 to 15 days.

We may point out that this is a very keen quotation and we trust that after consideration you will feel justified in placing the order with us. It will have our prompt attention.

Yours faithfully,

Encs.

Type the following exercise, inserting the correction signs in ink.

PROOF CORRECTION MARKS

caps. / Change letters underlined thrice to capital letters.

s.c. / Change letters underlined twice to small capital letters.

ital. / Change letters underlined once to italic letters.

rom. / Change letters underlined once to Roman (upright) letters.

l.c. / Change letters crossed through to lower case (small letters).

bold / Change letters underlined with wavy line to bold face.

trs. ⌉ Transpose matter as marked.

⊙ Insert full stop (full point).

⸍ Insert comma.

⸴ Insert semi-colon.

⸥ Insert inverted commas.

⸡ Insert superior figure (or letter).

⸠ Insert inferior figure (or letter).

Insert space.

eq. # Equalize the spacing.

N. P Start new paragraph with word after the bracket, [.

run on / No new paragraph. "Run on" the paragraph joined with line.

∂ Delete.

✗ Damaged letter. Substitute good letter.

☌ Letter "upside down." Turn letter right way up.

⊥ Push down space.

⌐ Move to the left.

¬ Move to the right.

‖ Straighten lines; type edge ragged.

═ Straighten lines; type unevenly set.

☐ Indent the first word.

⊃ / Take out space and close up.

∧ Insert the matter written in margin.

|-| Insert hyphen.

stet. "Let it stand"; ignore the correction dotted underneath.

u.c. / Change letters crossed through to upper case (capital letters).

Take a carbon copy of each of the following exercises,
inserting the date.

Margin stops: Pica 15 and 70; Elite 24 and 79

Line-space lever for single-line spacing.

Exercise 86

DK/JR

Messrs. Percy Miller & Co.,
15 Burnett Street,
London WC2H 7DT

Dear Sirs,

With reference to your Order A74 for best gas coke and our representative's interview with your secretary yesterday, we regret that, owing to the conditions prevailing at the present time, we are not in a position to arrange for our carmen to undertake the delivery of this quantity of coke unless they are paid an extra allowance for the long carry.

We are, however, pleased to accept your suggestion that you should pay us an extra 15p per tonne (i.e. 30p per load) and we shall arrange to give to the carmen an extra payment of 19p per tonne for the additional labour involved.

In accordance with this arrangement we propose to charge you for this particular delivery £24 per tonne.

We hope that these terms will be acceptable to you.

Yours faithfully,

Exercise 87

ADV/91

The Manager,
Carter, Bell & Co.,
Waverley Printing Works,
Edinburgh EH16 4AN

Dear Sir,

Kipling at one time used the word "Empusa" and a lively discussion was aroused as to its meaning. Every dictionary was dumb about it, until someone suggested looking in the NEW STANDARD DICTIONARY, and there it was!

This is typical of the NEW STANDARD DICTIONARY. It contains any and every word you may wish to find, and it becomes indispensable in the office.

No less than four hundred specialists compiled the Dictionary, so that its information is absolutely reliable. In addition to the usual dictionary information the NEW STANDARD contains the technical terms of every trade, all information about weights and measures, coinage, duties, loans, etc., and the thousand and one business details that crop up at a minute's notice. It has the value of a concise, accurate, business encyclopedia.

The work is in two handsome volumes. We shall be pleased to send you a booklet giving further detailed information about them or, if you prefer, we shall be glad to send them direct to your office for one week's examination free of charge or obligation to purchase.

Yours very truly,
T. W. Brown
Sales Manager

Exercise 88

Your ref: CD/prl/7
Our ref: LLS/Order 7496/b

Burslem, Hope & Co. Ltd.,
Burslem House,
Nettleton Square,
Wolverhampton, Staffs. WV6 7HG

For the attention of Mr. Charles Dodge

Dear Sirs,

Following last Monday's visit of your representative, Mr. Frank Edwards, we have decided to place with you an order for eight of your 3·6 m by 2·4 m pre-fabricated wooden huts (FRL/82/B), complete with floors, at a cost of £200 each. Full details are set out on the attached order form.

We should be grateful if you could deliver the first two of these huts before 8th December, as they are urgently needed for use on construction sites where work is beginning on 10th December. Mr. Edwards considered that delivery would be possible by that date.

Should the huts prove satisfactory, there is every possibility that a further dozen will be required. We should like to know whether you would consider granting a special discount on these.

Yours faithfully,

L. L. Stansbury

Director

Enc.

MANUSCRIPT WORK AND PROOF CORRECTION

Before beginning to type a piece of manuscript work, read it carefully to make sure you understand it. Pay particular attention to Exercise 153. The correction signs in it are used universally.

Exercise 152

HYPHENS.

A hyphen is a little thing, but it may mean a great deal. For example the notice we saw recently in a shop window, "Umbrellas Recovered", suggested that if you had lost your umbrella, you might recover it upon applying inside! This, however, was not the intention of the shopkeeper, who was merely asking you to let him have your shabby umbrella so that it might be re-covered.

In another connection the words recreation and re-creation were confused, and also remark and re-mark.

It is not always easy to decide about the use of a hyphen, and much depends upon popular custom and upon the exact shade of meaning it is intended to convey. Well-established words containing two complete words, such as nobleman, cupboard, bathroom, drop their hyphens, but it should be noted that dining-room retains the hyphen in order to avoid mispronunciation.

When one syllable of a word ends and the next begins with the same letter, the hyphen should be used to show that they are to be pronounced separately, e.g., co-operation, re-engage, pre-eminent, shell-less. Common-sense should either appear with a hyphen or as separate words. When it is hyphenated it becomes an adjective, as in the phrase "A common-sense proposition"; otherwise the words should be written separately, e.g. "He has plenty of common sense". When an adjective is expressed by a phrase, care should be taken to insert the hyphens, e.g. "a ten-year-old son".

Circulating Carbon Copies

When it is necessary to send carbon copies to persons other than the addressee many business houses request that the abbreviation "cc." shall be typed at the foot of letter followed by the names of the other recipients. This line usually appears on the top copy of the letter and on all carbon copies to make certain that everyone is aware of the distribution.

If it is desired that the addressee should not be informed of copies being sent to others, the abbreviation b.cc. (blind copy) should appear on the carbon copies only.

Take two carbon copies of each of the following exercises,
inserting suitable references and the date when these are not given.

Margin stops: Pica 12 and 72; Elite 20 and 80
Tab. stop: 17 or 26
Change left-hand margin stop to 22 or 32 for Exercise 90 when displaying list.

Line-space lever for single-line spacing.

Exercise 89

The Manageress,
Maison Lucille,
20 Westminster Palace Road,
London E17 8DJ

Dear Madam,

We wish to inform you that we have recently appointed Mr. Douglas Adams, of 59 Druce Avenue, Herne Hill, as our London Representative in succession to Mr. W. R. Norton, who has now left our service.

Mr. Adams will have pleasure in calling upon you in the near future, when we trust it will be convenient for you to grant him an interview.

He has been brought up in the Drapery Trade, and we feel sure you will find him able to give you valuable advice concerning the most suitable lines to be stocked for the coming season.

We enclose a supply of envelopes and postcards addressed to Mr. Adams, in order that, should you wish to see him specially at any time, you may be able to communicate with him direct.

We hope that his appointment may be to our mutual advantage, and that we shall continue to receive your orders for any goods that you require.

Yours faithfully,

Marion Green

Marketing Dept.

cc. Mrs. T. Roffe, Accounts Dept.

Encs.

Exercise 90

1st December, 19—

The Manager,
Corders Store,
44 Central Parade,
Eastbourne, Sussex EH8 7QR

Dear Sir,

You are cordially invited to our Spring Fashion Show which will be held in our Showroom at 101 Walton Street, Brighton, on Tuesday and Wednesday, 23rd and 24th January, at 1500 hrs.

The range shown will include:—
Boutique for the "Under Twenties"
Ladies' spring suits and dresses
New season's hats
Holiday and Cruise equipment
Exciting swimwear
Children's outfits
Leisure wear for the family
Men's wear—casual and formal
Flattering clothes for the "Over 40s"
Light-weight rainwear

Would you please let us know whether you will be attending one of these two shows, so that we may reserve seating for you.

Yours faithfully,

WEST END STYLES LTD.

Sales Director

cc. Mr A. J. R. Sorensen—Men's wear

Exercise 149

B. & T. MARSDEN (SPORTS OUTFITTERS) LTD.
Sales by Overseas Branches for Last Year

Branches	Summer Sports Wear	Winter Sports Wear	Sports Equipment
	£	£	£
France	5,623	3,426	10,962
Germany (West)	4,926	4,628	12,621
Sweden	3,126	5,127	9,187
Switzerland	2,121	12,621	3,121

Exercise 150

Display as clearly as possible the information given below.

Cartwright Plastics Ltd.

Expansion: 40% in last complete year; 140% since 1972.

Year ended 30th April	1973	1974	1975	1976
	£	£	£	£
Shareholders' Funds at beginning of year	5,892,000	9,362,000	9,877,000	10,387,000
Group Profit before Tax	1,433,000	1,657,000	2,137,000	2,583,000
Available for Ordinary Shareholders (net)	797,000	854,000	1,125,000	1,392,000
Net Dividend paid to Ordinary Shareholders	368,000	483,000	579,000	579,000

Exercise 151

Outlook for Next Year. The year has opened well and we face next year with confidence. Our efforts will continue to be directed towards efficient expansion at home and abroad. Next year, in the absence of special circumstances, progress should be maintained.

Figures for this year are as follows:–

	This Year	Last Year	Increase
Sales	£11,546,942	£9,341,032	23·6%
Profit before tax	£2,202,415	£1,740,211	26·5%
Tax	£1,240,868	£927,077	33·5%
Profit after tax	£961,547	£813,134	18·2%
Ordinary dividend (less tax)	30% £354,511	25% £302,816	17·1%
Cover for ordinary dividend	2·6 times	2·6 times	—
Unappropriated profit	£580,977	£484,562	19·9%
Net assets	£6,196,365	£5,302,076	16·9%

Letters Containing Headings

The following exercises give practice in the typing of headings.

If your machine is fitted with pica type, you can type ten characters to one inch. This means that on a sheet of A4 or A5 paper, 8¼ in (210 mm) wide, you can type 82 characters or spaces (with elite type you can type 99 characters or spaces).

In order to centre a heading on the sheet of typewriting paper, count the number of characters and spaces in the heading. In Exercise 91, there are 18 characters and spaces in the heading *158 Morecambe Road*. Subtract this number from the number of characters and spaces that you can type across the sheet of typewriting paper (82 − 18 = 64). If the heading is to be centred on the paper, half of these 64 spaces will have to be left before the heading, and half of them after the heading. Therefore divide 64 by 2 (= 32) and begin to type the heading at point 32 of the scale.

An alternative method of centring is to set the carriage at the centre of the scale (41 pica and 50 elite) and then back-space once for each two letters and spaces that the typed line will occupy (ignore any odd letter) and begin typing at the point to which you have back-spaced.

If you wish to centre the heading to the *writing line*, add the left and right margins and divide their total by two. For example with margins at 20 and 70, the centre of the writing line is 90 ÷ 2 = 45.

Use one of these methods for centring the headings in the remainder of the exercises. If the margins are uneven you must centre to the writing line.

Paragraph headings, such as those in Exercise 92, are often typed in capital letters.

Exercise 91

Margin stops: Pica 19 and 69: Elite 30 and 80

Line-space lever for single-line spacing.

BS/NF   15th January, 19--

Messrs. Pearsall & Flint,
58 Appletree Causeway,
Manningham,
Bradford, Yorkshire,
BD10 0PH

Dear Sirs,

158 Morecambe Road

From time to time we have had the pleasure of carrying out minor repairs at your existing premises, and we believe these have given you entire satisfaction.

We understand that you have just acquired the above premises, and we should be greatly obliged if you would allow us to submit an estimate for carrying out any alterations which you may find it necessary to make in order to render the premises suitable for your business.

We make a speciality of heating and lighting installations, and have also had considerable experience in the fitting of private inter-office telephones. We have just completed a large contract for this class of work for the Mildhall Manufacturing Co., whose premises are quite near to yours.

Your orders will receive our prompt and careful attention.

Yours faithfully,
for BURTON, MARCH & CO. LTD.

CITY ASSURANCE GROUP
PENSION BENEFITS

		At age 60		At age 65		At age 70
Age at entry	Premiums paid	Initial pension p.a.	Premiums paid	Initial pension p.a.	Premiums paid	Initial pension p.a.
	£	£	£	£	£	£
25	3,500	2,347	4,000	4,131	4,500	7,443
30	3,000	1,495	3,500	2,660	4,000	4,825
35	2,500	936	3,000	1,695	3,500	3,108
40	2,000	569	2,500	1,061	3,000	1,980
45	1,500	328	2,000	646	2,500	1,241
50	1,000	170	1,500	373	2,000	755
55	500	67	1,000	194	1,500	437
60	—	—	500	77	1,000	228

FEMALE The Pension will be these proportions of the male pensions:

$91\frac{3}{4}\%$ $89\frac{1}{2}\%$ $87\frac{1}{4}\%$

Exercise 148

Set out the Draft Statement of Accounts given below (as at 31st December, 19—).

Liabilities	£		Current Assets	£
Capital (in £1 Units of Stock):			Cash at Bank and in Hand	6,073,130
Authorized	10,000,000		Bills Discounted *less* Rebate and Reserve:	
			British Government	
Issued	7,500,000		Treasury Bills £114,662,154	
Reserve	4,000,000		Commercial and Other	
			Bills 62,532,864	
	11,500,000			177,195,018
Profit and Loss: Balance carried forward	769,066		Securities at less than Market Value:	
			British Government and Corporation Securities and British	
	12,269,066		Local Authority Bonds £107,575,589	
Loans Secured on Assets of the Company £279,710,090			British Corpn. and Public Bond Mortgages and Local	
Deposits, Other Liabilities and Reserve for Contingencies 17,163,374			Authority Bonds 7,012,399	
Deposits by Subsidiaries 100,107				114,587,988
Proposed Final Dividend less Income Tax 287,110			Loans and Amount Receivable	11,423,504
	297,260,681			309,279,640
			Fixed Assets	
			Shares in Subsidiaries at Cost	100,107
			Freehold Premises, including Furniture and Fittings, at Cost, *less* Amounts Written off	150,000
	£309,529,747			£309,529,747

Exercise 92

DKJ/BFT   5th January 19--

W. N. Beresford, Esq., M.A.,
Chorley House,
Brockenhurst, Hants.
SO4 7ZB

Dear Sir,

<u>26 Ebury Road, Barton</u>

We thank you for your letter of 2nd January.

We have on our estate at Barton several small houses
for sale, and we have pleasure in offering the following
property for your consideration:-

POSITION. The house is situated in Ebury Road, and
stands on a plot 15.2 m wide and 76.2 m deep. It stands
15.2 m back from the road, and this gives the opportunity
for the development of a beautiful front-garden approach to
the entrance.

ACCOMMODATION. The ground floor consists of a small
lounge-hall; dining-room and drawing-room, both about 3.4 m
by 4.6 m; and a large kitchen and laundry-room combined.
The upper floor contains four bedrooms, bathroom and lavatory.
There are fitted hand-basins in the two principal bedrooms.
Central heating throughout. Garage.

PRICE. The house, complete with freehold land, is
£25,000 and you might, if you wished, leave two-thirds of
this amount on mortgage, to be repaid over any reasonable
period.

We should be glad to show you over the house by appointment, and to give you any further particulars you may require.

Yours truly,
BURD & PERKINS LTD.

S. Burd
Director

Balance Sheets and Financial Statements

Re-read the notes on page 54 before you start to type the following exercises

Exercise 144

LIABILITIES

		£
Capital authorized and issued:–		
250,000 "A" shares of £20 each (£5 paid) . . .		5,000,000
500,000 "B" shares of £1 each fully paid		500,000
		5,500,000
Less uncalled on "A" shares		3,750,000
Paid up		1,750,000
Reserve Fund		1,125,000
Deposits		43,711,677
Dividend and bonus, payable 3rd January, 19— . .		87,500
Notes in circulation		3,874,263
Acceptances and other obligations		1,083,325
Drafts, circular notes, and other liabilities . . .		1,042,286
Profit and loss account		57,817
		£52,731,868

Exercise 145

UNIT TRUSTS

	Bid p	Offer p	Yield %
Abacus Growth	27½	29	3.20
Allied High Income	30	31½	5.56
Barclays Unicorn Trustee	71½	76	4.12
Castle Balanced	45	47½	7.50
Ebor High Return	54	57	6.61
Hodge Export Industries	24	25½	2.82
Investment-Assured Midlander ..	21½	23	4.28
London Wall Export Priority ..	26½	28½	3.80
M. & G. Magnum	124	128	2.78
National Security First	51	54	4.41
Save and Prosper Income	28½	30	6.35

Exercise 146

STATEMENT OF ACCOUNT for Year Ended 31st March, 19—

Expenditure	£	Income	£
Rent	21·20	Balance brought forward	102·50
Rates	12·15	Grants from London	162·30
Delegate's Expenses	17·40	Interest on £200 National War	
Membership Cards	4·50	Bond	10·00
Printing	10·75	Bank Interest	2·75
Hire of Rooms	14·95		
Caretaker	20·50		
Sundries	6·14		
	107·59		
Balance in hand	169·96		
	£277·55		£277·55

Display the following letters on A4 paper.

Take one carbon copy of each letter and insert today's date.

Use fully-blocked and open-punctuated style.

Exercise 93

The Secretary
Mercury Cycle Co Ltd
Chesterfield Road
Sheffield S8 PRY

Dear Sir
Our Ref GE 6562

We have pleasure in bringing to your notice our new Desk Autograph which we are offering at the very reasonable price of £25.

For some considerable period there has been a demand for a small time recorder for registering the arrival and departure of staff and salesmen, but owing to the high cost of wages and materials we have not until now been able to make a machine that would meet the demand. As a result of experience covering more than two years we have been able to construct a thoroughly reliable machine and to simplify the mechanism so that we could bring the machine on the market at a price that would ensure a ready sale. In the first place, we would not put our name to a machine unless it could be supplied with a thoroughly reliable time-piece. The clock movement is made throughout in our own works, with the exception of the balance wheel and lever escapement, which contain specialized Swiss parts. We are fitting the finest escapement that it is possible to procure; hence good time-keeping is guaranteed, and the printing and operating mechanism are of the high-class quality for which we are famous. We can, therefore, confidently recommend this Desk Autograph as a machine that will give you efficient service for very many years.

In order to enable you to test the value of this silent force in ensuring the punctuality of your employees, we shall be glad to send one or more of these Desk Autographs on a month's free trial.

Yours faithfully

JOHN HALE SONS & CO

Supervisor GE Dept

Exercise 94

ADV/24

Messrs Thomas Roby & Sons
23 Selborne Chambers
Old Broad Street London E17 8PA

Dear Sirs
The "Super" Clasp

We have pleasure in bringing to your notice the "SUPER" CLASP, and we enclose leaflets depicting the clasp and detailing a few of the many uses to which it may be applied.

The "SUPER" CLASP is an indispensable office requisite. It is one of the neatest little time-savers and desk companions for clerks, cashiers, accountants and business men generally. It supersedes the use of rubber bands and paper weights. It is designed to take from one to 200 sheets or more, and to hold them securely. It is made in one piece, of the finest quality clock spring steel, treated, and is guaranteed to retain its position under all ordinary usage. It is unbreakable and lasts for ever.

The "SUPER" CLASP is a great convenience wherever there are papers to be handled. Although this little contrivance has been on the market only a month or so, it is meeting with remarkable popularity far and wide.

We have pleasure in quoting you the following prices:–

A sample 10 for £0·70
          30   £2·00
          150   £6·00 net. Delivered free.

Yours faithfully

Sales Manager

Encs

Exercise 140

MEMORANDUM

To   All Sales Representatives   9 October 19—

From Sales Manager

Weekly Reports

As requested at last month's sales conference a new style of weekly report form has been ordered from the printer. A supply will be sent to you within the next ten days.

The layout of the new report form should prove easier to read and time-saving to complete.

Exercise 141

MEMORANDUM

27 February 19—

To   Branch Managers

From Manager, Salaries Dept.

From next month all salary details will be fed into our new computer.

Please notify me by the 14th of each month the number of hours worked by the part-time members of your staff and their rates of pay.

Exercise 142

MEMORANDUM

To   Manager, Nottingham Office

From Head Office

STOCKTAKING

Please arrange to list all items of stock held at your office on 31st March 19—

Miss J. S. Robins will arrive at 0900 hours on 31st March 19— to help you with the stocktaking. She will bring with her the current price list and a supply of stock sheets.

Annual Audit

All account books must be closed at 31st March 19— and a list of balances prepared for the Chief Accountant's visit to your office next month.

2 March 19—
Ref SA/23

Exercise 143

MEMORANDUM

From: M A Kippen, General Manager   Date: 8 April 19—

To: All Managers

Subject: New Bar Prices

The enclosed price lists are to be introduced into the relevant bars of the hotel on Sunday, April 11th 19—.

They include certain backdated increases from breweries and of course the recent budget increases. They are to be displayed in prominent positions and any adjustments for future increases will be notified to you by means of a new list.

Enc.

c.c. Stocktaker

64

Exercise 95

PRB/MC

James Maxwell, Esq.,
15 Bank Chambers,
Shrewsbury SY5 65B

Dear Sir,

Mr. James Good

This is to introduce Mr. James Good, a customer at this branch, who wishes to purchase a house at Croydon, Surrey, and would be glad if you would act on his behalf in this matter.

The vendor's solicitors are Messrs. Wilson and Harding, of 8 The Broadway, Sutton, Surrey, and we have informed them that you are acting for Mr. Good.

The proposed purchase price is £15,000 and the settlement date is 31st March 19—. The property has been viewed by our representative and seems quite satisfactory at the proposed figure.

For our requirements, we shall be obliged if you will make the necessary searches both in the local Land Charges Register and in the Official Land Charges Register, and also confirm that there are no adverse entries in the Town and Country Planning Act.

Our customer is taking a loan of £3,500 on this property, and we are therefore enclosing our Form of Charge, which we shall be obliged if you will kindly have completed and returned to us with the relative deeds of the property.

Yours faithfully,

Enc.

Exercise 96

Messrs. Bretton & Bell,
15 Shaw Road West,
Leicester LE2 8UN

Dear Sirs,

Sports and Pastimes—AD496

Not having had the pleasure of hearing from you about reservation of advertising space in "Sports and Pastimes," we venture once again to bring this important advertising medium to your notice.

During the early part of September our readers will realize that summer will soon be at an end and will then be thinking out their plans for the winter. This means many new purchases, which put a substantial amount of new business in the way of advertisers.

Advertisers wishing to share in this business should have their advertisements before the readers early, and we shall be pleased to reserve space for you, beginning with next month's issue.

Advertising rates are:–

£12 per page for 1 insertion
£11 „   „   per insertion for   3 insertions
£10 „   „   „   „   „   6   „
£8 „   „   „   „   „   12   „

We are prepared to book half, quarter, and one-eighth page spaces at proportionate rates.

Please let us have instructions within the next seven days.

Yours faithfully,

Exercise 97

The Secretary,
Broadley & Town Ltd.,
Radlett Works,
London WC1N 2LS

Dear Sir,

Fire Insurance—Ref: 49A/24/Rad

Following the conversation with you today, we are attaching hereto a draft specification, together with a copy of our plan.

The amounts appearing against items 7–10, which are, of course, to be taken without prejudice, are those suggested by our surveyor. If possible we should like divisions of amounts in respect of items 1–4, which we propose including in cancellation of policies Nos. 2196754 and 2387652.

We understand that the building adjoining D, D1 and D2, and also the detached stable near to this building, are the property of Messrs. Smalley & Jones, but these are not included in the insurance.

We shall be glad if you will return the draft specification after examination, and at the same time inform us of the suggested amounts for each of items 1–4.

Yours faithfully,

Encs. 2.

Exercise 138

Messrs. A. & L. Higginson, 12 Station Parade, Ormskirk L30 3SG			10th June, 19—
Bought of THE IDEAL HARDWARE CO. LTD.			

		£	£
2 No. 256 Ideal Baths 1·7 m	@ 33·50 each		67·00
3 No. 23 Lavatory Basins	@ 24·90 ,,		74·70
6 No. 3 Draining Boards	@ 3·20 ,,		19·20
6 No. 7 ,, ,,	@ 5·60 ,,		33·60
			£194·50

Exercise 139

Type the following invoices in the correct form, using today's date.

From R. Brace & Co. Ltd., 19 Molton Road, Leicester LE4 4GU
To J. O'Brien & Sons, 140 Hamilton Street, Manchester M10 6LF

			£	£
BR197B	4 doz. prs. shoes	@ 3·50 pr.		168·00
BR917T	4 doz. ,, ,,	@ 3·50 pr.		168·00
MF306F	3 doz. ,, ,,	@ 4·00 pr.		144·00
MF206W	3 doz. ,, ,,	@ 4·00 pr.		144·00
MF306N	2 doz. ,, ,,	@ 4·00 pr.		96·04
E812B	1 doz. ,, ,,	@ 6·00 pr.		72·00
E12O	1 doz. ,, ,,	@ 6·00 pr.		72·00
				£864·00

From J. R. Roberts & Sons, Cameron Works, Reading, Berks. RG4 7BT
To P. G. Latimer, 113 Croydon Road, Purley, Surrey CR2 4DE

		£	£
3 1·8-kg tins shortbread	@ 2·10 ea.		6·30
8 1·8-kg tins semi-sweet biscuits	@ 1·20 ea.		9·60
12 226-gm tins cocktail assorted	@ 0·20 ea.		2·40
			£18·30

Memorandums

A memorandum (or memo) is used for communication within an organization. A5 paper, with the longest dimension across the top, may be used for short messages. The style of layout may vary from firm to firm.

Type the following exercises taking a carbon copy of each.

Hanging Paragraphs

In a hanging paragraph the second and subsequent lines are indented two (or three) spaces from the first line. In the following exercises you will find it helpful to set two tabular stops—the first for the first line of each hanging paragraph, and the second for the second and subsequent lines.

Notice that the lines of the indented paragraphs finish about ½ in (13 mm) before the main right-hand margin. Change the left-hand margin stop for the second and subsequent lines of the hanging paragraphs, and use the margin release key when typing the first line. Change the right-hand margin stop for the indented right-hand margin. Remember to re-set the margin stops when you have completed the last hanging paragraph.

Exercise 98

Margin stops: Pica 12 and 72: Elite 21 and 81

Line-space lever for single-line spacing.

7th May, 19--

The Rev. Sinclair Lewis, D.D.,
The Vicarage,
Bromley, Kent,
BR1 2NA

Dear Sir,

Thank you very much for allowing me to see the plan and draft specification of the joint garage.

The following points occur to me:-

(1) There does not appear to be any provision made for ventilation. This, I think, is important, as in the absence of ventilation in wet or damp weather there would be considerable sweating, and rust would result.

(2) The hinges of the front doors should be of wrought or cast iron, and should allow the doors to be lifted off when open.

(3) The match-boarding of the doors would look better if the boards had a V finish.

(4) I suggest that the inside brick walls should be distempered. This does not appear to have been included in the specification.

(5) It would be an advantage if the fanlight over the back door could be made to open.

I think if these small items receive attention everything will be in order.

I return the plans and draft specification herewith.

Yours very truly,

Encs.

Exercise 136

<table>
<tr><td colspan="5" style="text-align:center">Bought of
MAISON NANATTE,
New Bond Street, London WiY 9LG</td></tr>
</table>

Bought of
MAISON NANATTE,
New Bond Street, London WiY 9LG

Miss E. R. Sweeting,
26 Medusa Road,
Nottingham
NGL 9LZ

8th September, 19--

				£
8 m	Crimplene	90 cm	@ £2.99	23.92
3 "	Dress Lace	115 cm	@ £5.85	17.55
12 "	Polyester Cotton	137 cm	@ £1.25	15.00
9 "	Nylon	150 cm	@ £1.50	13.50
12 "	Terry Towelling	137 cm	@ £1.25	15.00
12 "	Tricel	90 cm	@ £2.25	27.00
7 "	Voile	115 cm	@ £2.50	17.50
				£129.47

Exercise 137

Messrs. Parker & O'Neil,   15th June, 19—
25 St. Mary's Road,
Ludlow, Salop. SY8 3LY
Bought of THE ACME WIRELESS SUPPLY CO.

	£	£
2 doz. Valve Holders	@ 1·19 per doz.	2·38
3 "Tyrol" Condensers	@ 1·62 each	4·86
36 Lead-in Tubes	@ 1·50 per doz.	4·50
130 m Lead-in Wire	@ 0·40 per metre	52·00
6 Condenser Dials	@ 0·24 each	1·44
3 prs. No. 6 Headphones	@ 1·97 each	5·91
		£71·09

Type the following letters for signature.

Take two carbon copies of Exercise 99 and mark one carbon for Mr. Richard Ashworth. Make three carbon copies of Exercise 100 marking one for Mrs. Barbara Reid—Publicity Department and one for Mr. Nigel Ballard—Marketing Services.

Margin stops: Pica 15 and 70; Elite 24 and 79

Line-space lever for single-line spacing.

Exercise 99

Your ref: DP/LR　　　　　　　7th May, 19—
Our ref: REP/82

Messrs. Parker, Coles & Co.
The Central Estate Office,
3 Park Road,
Leicester LE5 5DV

Dear Sirs,

<u>2 Granville Gardens</u>

We were called in last Wednesday to attend to stoppages and water supplies, and the following work was executed :–

Opening up ground in garden, cutting out defective pipe and sealing off pipe.
Taking out obsolete plug cock in cellar and wiping in new 18 mm union stop cock.
Taking out defective ball valve in storage tank and fixing new one.
Clearing air-locked pipe from storage tank in roof.

The cause of the tank pipe's becoming air-locked is that the storage tank is too small to hold sufficient water to supply the washbasins, without at times being quite empty and allowing the passage of air into the draw-off pipe, and also that the service pipe has many dips in it.

To obviate the trouble and ensure a good supply to the washbasins, we suggest that another 182-litre tank should be fixed in the roof.

Yours faithfully,

General Manager

Exercise 100

SPA/81　　　　　　　　　　8th July, 19—

Colin Edmundsen, Esq.,
The Advertising Manager,
The Belton Paint Co. Ltd.,
Hand Court, London WC1R 5HP

Dear Mr. Edmundsen,

Following our conversation on advertising mediums last Saturday I shall now do my best to persuade you that Press advertising, particularly in a newspaper such as the "Sunday Leader," is not only the most effective medium but is also undoubtedly the best value for money.

May I show you the advantages of "Sunday Leader" advertising and summarize them as follows :–

(1) An illustrated Sunday newspaper with strong "home" interests is read by every member of the household.
(2) A net sale of 2,000,000 copies ensures that your advertisements reach a wide section of the public.
(3) A newspaper that arrives in the home on Sunday morning when everyone has some leisure for reading will receive more attention than a daily newspaper.
(4) A paper of handy size can be read without folding and the consequent turning back of advertisers' announcements.
(5) The advertising rate of £500 per column, or 25p per 1,000 net sales, is not prohibitive for the small advertiser.

I suggest that these are weighty reasons why you should consider the "Sunday Leader" as an advertising medium and would like the opportunity of discussing your requirements in greater detail.

Yours sincerely,

S. P. Atkins

Advertisement Manager

Invoices

Invoices are usually typed on special headed paper, the size of which varies from firm to firm. They may be typed in single- or double-line spacing. Re-read the notes on page 54 before you start to type and rule the following exercises.

When typing columns of money in decimal currency the libra sign (£) should be positioned at the top of the column over the decimal points. This practice gives the best result from a "balance" and display point of view.

Exercise 134

		£	£
Mr. W. Paterson,   8th August, 19—
21 High Street,
Beckenham,
BR1 0RL

Bought of WILSON & SQUIRES

					£	£
3 prs.	Quality A3 Blankets			@	7·35	22·05
2	„	„	Ax Guest Towels	@	2·40	4·80
3	„	Cotton Sheets, 2 m by 3 m		@	3·90	11·70
2	„	Twill „ 2·25 m by 3 m		@	2·90	5·80
						£44·35

Exercise 135

Colton Works,
Barnes E4 7RG

Messrs. Jarvis Brothers,   11th July, 19—
94 High Street,
Northampton
NN3 4DT

Dr. to STOKES & MONTAGUE LTD.

Terms: 2½% one month.

			£	£
June	1	To Goods		38·97
	5	„ „		53·47
	7	„ „		88·11
	9	By Returns	3·32	
	12	To Goods		37·11
	14	„ „		13·60
	18	„ „		55·50
	22	By Allowance	1·50	
	25	To Goods		32·79
	28	„ „		56·11
				375·66
				4·82
				£370·84

Letters on A5 Paper

Type the following exercises twice—on A5 paper, 210 × 149 mm, and on A5 paper, turned sideways 149 × 210 mm. Insert the date of typing when this is not given.

Margin stops (8¼ × 5⅞ in (210 × 149 mm)): Pica 15 and 70; Elite 24 and 79
Margin stops (5⅞ × 8¼ in (149 × 210 mm)): Pica 12 and 50; Elite 18 and 60

Line-space lever for single-line spacing.

Exercise 101

DBK/SL

R. J. Norten, Esq., B.Sc.,
Electricitas Ltd.,
High Street,
Hull, Yorkshire HU6 9SY

Dear Sir,

This letter confirms our telegram of today as follows: "Endeavour dispatch headphones tomorrow. Stock exhausted."

We should like to remind you that these headphones were placed on order nearly three weeks ago, and you promised speedy delivery. Several of our customers threaten to cancel their orders, and we trust that there will be no further delay.

Yours truly,
SIMPSON & BARRETT

Exercise 102

The Manager,
The Commodore Motor Garage,
Palace Road,
Bromley BR2 6DQ

Dear Sir,

Inspection of Car XL 269

We regret that we are unable to trace the receipt of particulars of the inspection of the above car, which took place two months ago. As these are required for our auditors, we shall be greatly obliged if you will please forward us a duplicate of the original.

Yours faithfully,

Assistant Manager

Exercise 103

7th August, 19—

Monsieur Jules Lestrange,
Pension des Alpes,
Berne,
Switzerland.

Dear Sir,

Policy 926541

In response to your letter of 4th August, enclosing the above policy, we regret to inform you that we cannot allow any return of premium in this instance.

We shall be pleased to quote for the insurance of your new car upon your return to England. If you will kindly inform us upon your arrival, we shall arrange for one of our representatives to call and see you.

Yours faithfully,

Manager

Exercise 104

Your ref: ABR/sm   2nd January, 19—
Our ref: BK/LD

Messrs. John Brown & Co.,
56 Loates Lane,
Manchester M1 7JG

Dear Sirs,

We thank you for your letter of 1st January. Before we approach underwriters for quotations, we should be glad if you would kindly furnish us with the following information:–

(1) Average size of shipments.
(2) Principal ports of destination.
(3) Previous experience of claims made during the last three years.

We feel sure that with this information we shall be able to show you some improvements on your present rates.

Yours faithfully,

45

Exercise 132

Set the appropriate margins for A4 paper to give a balanced display to the following notice of an extraordinary general meeting.

THE SOUTH LANCASHIRE TRADING COMPANY LIMITED

NOTICE IS HEREBY GIVEN that an EXTRAORDINARY GENERAL MEETING of this Company will be held at the Registered Offices, 37 Dale Street, Manchester, on Friday, 3rd March, 19—, at 1500 hrs, when the subjoined resolution which was passed at the Extraordinary General Meeting of the Company, held on 15th day of February, 19—, will be submitted for confirmation as a Special Resolution:–

"That the Articles of Association be altered in the following manner:–
"By striking out and cancelling the words 'in case of shares not fully paid up' where such words appear in Article 47."

Dated the 23rd day of February, 19—.
By Order of the Board,
THOMAS MASSEY,
Secretary
37 Dale Street,
Manchester M1 3LQ

Exercise 133

The following notice is typical of notices sent out by estate agents. Capitalization is important and careful consideration should be given to this aspect of display. In the office situation a stencil would be prepared so that duplicated copies could be circulated to interested clients.

When typing a stencil remember to disengage the ribbon, clean the type faces, and use an even touch.

Special care is necessary when checking stencils (or other masters used for duplicating processes), and for this purpose the carbon paper behind stencils is reversed. If corrections need to be made, a pencil should be placed between the stencil and carbon paper, correcting fluid applied and allowed to dry before removing the pencil and typing in the correction.

The stencil should be proof-read while it is still in the typewriter. To avoid missing errors it is wise to enlist the aid of another typist who can check the typing as it is read from the original copy.

Exercise 133 (continued)

NORTH LONDON

Situated high up in a good class residential district six or seven minutes' walk from the Central Station, close to the Heath and within easy reach of Golders Green Station.

The Freehold Residence, known as:–

"THE FOLLIES"
Berkhampstead Road

A house of interesting appearance, built of red brick, with mullioned lattice windows on the ground floor, with black and white half-timber work above (some finely carved). Gabled red-tiled roof.

It stands well back from the road approached by a gravelled drive and contains the following accommodation:–

Hall: about 3·7 m square with panelled dado and front door having carved panels.

Drawing Room: 5·8 m by 6·7 m with panelled dado and elaborate ceiling and mantel, with an annexe 6·1 m by 3·0 m (formerly a separate room) at a higher level.

Dining Room: about 10·7 m by 5·8 m exclusive of three deep bays—a magnificent apartment panelled in oak and having an oak parquet floor. The ceiling is traversed by heavy beams supported by stone corbels and the mantelpiece is also of oak with some interesting old carved panels.

The domestic offices, including kitchen, pantry, scullery, larder, are grouped conveniently apart from the reception rooms and are fitted with modern sinks, cookers, etc.

On the First Floor: Five bedrooms; bathroom and W.C.

On the Second Floor: Two large and two smaller bedrooms; bathroom.

Company's water, gas, and electric light are installed, and there is a central heating system.

Large sums have been spent upon the property in the past, and although it has not been occupied by the owner for some time and consequently stands in need of renovations it offers an opportunity of acquiring a place which, with a very small outlay, would provide a charming residence at a small fraction of its cost.

PRICE, with Vacant Possession, £65,000
(subject to formal contract)

Type exercises 105–8 on A5 paper, portrait (with the short dimension across the top). Take one carbon copy of each letter. If it is necessary to erase remember to move the typewriter carriage to the side, insert a piece of stiff card behind the front sheet and erase with circular movements.

Your carbon copies should be free of smudges. If your employer makes a handwritten correction when signing letters, and the letter is not to be retyped, it is important that you note this on the carbon copies before they are filed.

Exercise 105

5th July, 19—

The Manager,
National Bank Ltd.,
928 High Street,
Atherton M29 9JG

Dear Sir,

I do not appear to have received my usual quarterly statement which should have been sent to me on 30th June; and, as I am anxious to prepare my accounts for audit, I shall be glad if you will let me have this statement without delay.

Yours faithfully,

J. Jones

Exercise 106

Your ref: BP/RL
Our ref: Dem/51

3rd April, 19—

Messrs. James Dee & Sons,
47 High Street,
Havant, Hants.
Po9 4DH

Dear Sirs,

We thank you for your inquiry of 1st April, and shall be pleased to arrange for one of our representatives to call at your office to give you a demonstration of our new electric typewriter.

If you will kindly let us know a date that would be convenient to you, we shall then be able to make the necessary arrangements.

Yours faithfully,

Sales Manager

Exercise 107

7th January, 19—

The Printers' Inn,
52 Dering Street,
London W1R 9AB

Attention of Mr. Bridges

Dear Sirs,

I am writing to confirm that I should be grateful if you would reserve your Banqueting Room for us for the evening of Tuesday, 10th March, as arranged today on the telephone.

I look forward to receiving details of menus and prices from you.

Yours faithfully,

Sales Manager

Exercise 108

14th April, 19—

Benson Hire Car Service,
41 Berkeley Street,
London W1X 5AB

Dear Sirs,

American clients of ours, Mr. Albert Grossen and his wife, will be requiring a chauffeur-driven Rolls-Royce for ten days from Saturday, 11th July, to visit Stratford-on-Avon and the Lake District. Would you please let us know if you are in a position to provide this service, and what your rate of charges would be.

Yours faithfully,
INTERNATIONAL TRAVELLERS

Manager

Type the following exercise on A5 paper.

Exercise 128

SPECIAL OFFER OF CARPETS

Length	Width	Price
		£
2·440 m	2·287 m	32·50
2·440 m	2·745 m	35·00
3·66 m	2·745 m	68·45
3·965 m	2·745 m	76·75
3·66 m	3·202 m	80·50
3·05 m	3·202 m	91·25
3·05 m	3·66 m	100·00

Use A4 paper for Exercises 129–31.

Exercise 129

4th June, 19—

The Directors,
Green Park Cinema,
Forest Gate, London E7 5BP

Dear Sirs,

In accordance with the particulars taken by our representative, we have pleasure in submitting the following estimate for the mosaic pavings:–

	£
Entrance Lobby and Sill. To provide, fix, and finish with fine sanded Roman cube marble mosaic paving, as sketch herewith, with ornamental border and white straight course filling, complete upon ready-prepared concrete foundation, for the sum of	47·00
Basement Stairs. To repair the mosaic paving at the top of the basement stairs in the central hall	12·50
Half Landing. To cut out and level up the existing granolithic floor where badly worn	12·00
	£71·50

We hope that this estimate will be acceptable to you, and look forward to hearing from you in the course of the next few days.

Yours faithfully,

Enc.

Exercise 130

5th August, 19—
The Secretary,
Universal Insurance Co. Ltd.,
59 Phoenix Road,
Edinburgh EH8 7BT

Dear Sir,

I have pleasure in enclosing the Wages Adjustment Statement in respect of Policy W.R. 45796, together with a cheque in payment of the amount due as excess premium, and also for the premium in respect of the Public Liability Policy, No. P.L. 837562. The amount is made up as follows:–

		£	£
For Policy W.R. 45796 (£33,000)			58·99
Less commission 15%			8·85
			50·14
Less amount already paid			38·59
			11·55
Policy P.L. 837562		7·00	
Less commission 15%		1·05	
			5·95
Cheque herewith			£17·50

I shall be glad to have your acknowledgement in due course.

Yours truly,

Encs.

Exercise 131

Our ref. 217/GS

J. R. Bruce, Esq.,
93 Long Lane,
Cheltenham GL50 2DT

Dear Sir,

With reference to your request for travellers' cheques for your visit to Malta next month, I have pleasure in enclosing these as follows:–

Travellers' cheques				£
3 valued £20 each	..	..	..	60
3 „ £10 „	..	..	..	30
1 „ £5 „	..	..	..	5
				£95

Your account has been debited with the above amount and with the cost of issuing the travellers' cheques (35p).

Yours faithfully,

Manager
Encs.

Official Letters

The layout of official letters recommended by the Civil Service is as follows:—

MARGINS: The left-hand margin is usually ¾ in (19 mm). The right-hand margin has at least two spaces.

REFERENCE: The printed letterhead is designed so that by setting one tabulation stop for the insertion of the telephone number, the same stop is used for the reference and date.

DATE: The date is typed as:— 1 March 1971.

NAME AND ADDRESS OF ADDRESSEE: As window envelopes will be used, the printed letterhead is designed with this fact in mind and guidance is given to the typist so that the name and address are correctly placed. The name of the town should be typed in capital letters. The style of punctuation used is normally referred to as "open punctuation" and this means omitting all punctuation marks except where ambiguity would result. Words such as Road, Street, etc., should not be abbreviated.

SALUTATION: For official letters, *Sir, Gentlemen, Madam*; for semi-official letters, *Dear Sir, Dear Madam, Dear Brown.*

PARAGRAPHS: Block method to be used.

COMPLIMENTARY CLOSE: For official letters *I am Sir Your obedient Servant:* for semi-official letters *Yours faithfully, Yours sincerely:* for Secretaries of State and Under Secretaries, *I have the honour to be Sir Your obedient Servant.* The complimentary close can be typed against the left-hand margin or the same tabulation stop as for references and date may be utilised.

HEADINGS: The headings should commence at the left-hand margin.

PUNCTUATION: The open method of punctuation is used; see Exercise 110 for example.

CONTINUATION SHEETS: The number of the page, the name of the addressee and the date are typed at the top of the page. In some Government departments the reverse side of the paper is used instead of a continuation sheet. The margins are reversed and the typing line is usually started at the position of the first line of the body of the letter on the first page.

Exercise 109

Margin stops: Pica 8 and 76: Elite 9 and 92 Tab. stop: 50 or 60

```
R S Brown Esq                          AB/EC
140 High Street
NEWPORT, Mon                           JR/PV/694C
NPT OEF
                                       1 October 19..


Dear Sir

IMPROVEMENT GRANTS

In reply to your inquiry, I enclose a copy of the Government publication "Improve
your House with a Grant".  I also enclose an application form for a standard or
discretionary grant together with a note of the conditions applicable to each.

Grants cannot be given for works of replacement of any worn out or obsolete ameni-
ties; these are classed as "repairs" and do not come within the scope of the Act.
If there is evidence that any of the standard amenities have existed at some time,
although they might have been removed prior to occupation by the applicant, the
Council cannot make a grant for their replacement.

                                       Yours faithfully



                                       Town Clerk
```

> Note that the Civil Service preference is for terminal punctuation to appear outside terminal quotation marks unless the punctuation is part of the quoted matter.

```
Encs
```

Exercise 125

MEMBERSHIP RETURN

	This Year	Last Year
Birmingham	124	134
Glasgow	146	147
Liverpool and District	109	105
Manchester	225	215
North-East Coast	128	127
Sheffield and District	96	98
South Wales	87	87
West Yorkshire	100	85
North-East Midlands	47	46
Bristol and District	45	—
South African	113	125
Australian (Sydney)..	225	260
Australian (Melbourne)	136	137
Australian (Brisbane)	72	63
Canadian (Montreal)	32	23
	1,685	1,652

Exercise 126

METRIC UNITS AND SYMBOLS

units	symbol	alternative for typists
metre	m	—
centimetre	cm	—
millimetre	mm	—
square metre	m^2	sq m
cubic metre	m^3	cu m
kilogram	kg	—
tonne(s)	tonne(s)	—
litre(s)	litre(s)	—
watt	W	—
kilogram per cubic metre	kg/m^3	kg/cu m
degree Celsius	°C	—

NOTE: No full stops are put after symbols, except at the end of a
sentence.
Symbols are the same in the singular as they are in the
plural except for tonne and litre.
Celsius is the new name for centigrade.

Exercise 127

Display the following information on a sheet of A5 paper

HOCKEY

Captain: M. J. Webb. Team: J. Barrett, M. Fordham, P. Heath, S. Kingsfield,
C. Lawson, R. Lorimer, M. Malone, W. Morris, O. Norris, S. Sinclair, F. Skelton,
D. Windsor.
Results: v. City 1—1 (draw, home); v. City Hospital 3—0 (won, away); v. B.H.S.
Old Girls 1—2 (lost, home); v. Old Collegians 2—2 (draw, home); v. City 3—1
(won, away); v. Windsor Ladies 1—1 (draw, away); v. Slough T.C. 5—1 (won,
home); v. Staines S.C. 2—1 (won, away).

A Shunter Esq   AS/MNO
Stationbury
DORSET   CC 586/52
PL18 9EG
                                        4 June 19--

Sir

COUNTY - DORSET

PLACE - STATIONBURY

A PORTER'S CHARITY

(PROPOSED SALE)

I return to you the draft conditions of sale which have been
examined in this office for the purpose of ascertaining that
the liability of the trustees in respect of the production of
title and otherwise is sufficiently restricted.

The Commissioners see no objection in this respect to the
conditions as now framed, for the technical sufficiency of
which, however, the legal advisers of the trustees remain
responsible.

Two copies of the particulars and conditions of sale should
be sent to this office as soon as they have been printed or
typed. These copies should be forwarded as soon as possible
and instructions relating to the reserved price will be sent
to you as soon as copies have been received.

I am Sir
Your obedient Servant

Assistant Commissioner

Exercise 122

Today's market displayed distinct steadiness, and a fair volume of business resulted. September buyers £1.15, October £1.14 to £1.15, December £1.12½ to £1.13, March £1.12½ to £1.45, May £1.14. The 1100 hrs "call" was as follows:–

			Sellers £	Buyers £
September	..	.. ..	1.16	1.12½
October	..	.. ..	1.16	1.15
November	..	.. ..	1.13	1.11
October–December	..	..	1.14	1.12½
January–March	..	..	1.14	1.13

Exercise 123

SIMPLE AND COMPOUND INTEREST

Table showing the number of years at which any principal doubles itself at the various rates of interest stated

Rate of Interest				Years at Simple Interest	Years at Compound Interest
2	..	..	..	.. 50	35.0027
2½	..	..	..	.. 40	28.0710
3	..	..	..	.. 33.3333	23.4497
3½	..	..	..	.. 28.5714	20.1487
4	..	..	..	.. 25	17.6729
4½	..	..	..	.. 22.2222	15.7473
5	..	..	..	.. 20	14.2066
6	..	..	..	.. 16.6666	11.8956
7	..	..	..	.. 14.2857	10.2447
8	..	..	..	.. 12.5	9.0064
9	..	..	..	.. 11.1111	8.0432
10	..	..	..	.. 10	7.2725

Exercise 124

WEST, HATFIELD AND COMPANY LIMITED

Sales of "Star" Transistor Radios for last year

MONTH	TYPE OF MODEL			
	Model A Standard	Model A Super	Model B Standard	Model B Super
January	15	13	18	15
February	18	18	23	17
March	25	27	38	21
April	17	28	28	36
May	18	21	26	34
June	15	18	15	21
July	13	20	13	15
August	11	25	19	19
September ..	17	31	26	41
October	18	37	28	46
November	21	25	30	54
December	17	32	24	49
Total	205	295	288	368

Type the following official letter on A4 paper leaving 2 in (50 mm) of clear space at the top. Take two carbon copies.

A Taxpayer Esq   CT/AG
10 Sheffield Place
LIVERPOOL   GL/WM/186
L6 3AA
                                            6 June 19--

Sir

With reference to your letter of 4 June, I am directed by the Board of Inland Revenue to say that where a person who has been ordinarily resident in the United Kingdom leaves to take up an employment exercised wholly abroad for a period which includes at least one complete Income Tax year (ending 5 April), he is regarded for Income Tax purposes as not resident in the United Kingdom for the period from the date of his departure to the date of his return to resume permanent residence here, except as follows:-

(a) If no place of abode is maintained available for his use in the United Kingdom, he is regarded as resident if the average time which he spends in this country amounts to three months in the year or more and for any Income Tax year in which he is in this country for a period or periods equal in the whole to six months.

(b) If a place of abode is maintained available for his use in the United Kingdom he is regarded as resident for any year in which he pays a visit (before his final return) of any length to this country.

For any year in which he is regarded as resident, his remuneration (assuming that it is normally paid abroad except for allotments to dependants in this country) is liable to United Kingdom Income Tax by reference to the amounts received in or remitted to this country (including such allotments).

I am Sir
Your obedient Servant

Leader Dots

When typing the following exercises, practise the use of leader dots, the purpose of which is to lead the eye from one point to another. The usual methods of displaying leader dots are:-

1. Two dots, three spaces   ..   ..   ..
2. Three dots, two spaces   ...   .
3. Continuous dots   ....

When typing leader dots in groups, they must be typed uniformly underneath each other. At least one space must always be left between the last word and the first leader dot and between the last leader dot and the following word or vertical line. Always insert the leader dots on each line as you type that line. Remember to type the dots lightly or they will pierce the paper.

After calculating the tabulations select paper of an appropriate size and type each of the following exercises.

Exercise 120

SINGLE-SUBJECT EXAMINATIONS

SUBJECT	RESULTS		
	Credit	Pass	Fail
Art	80	280	40
English	60	470	180
Shorthand	60	120	20
Typewriting Stage I	50	160	30
Typewriting Stage II	10	60	40

Exercise 121

MONTHLY GENERAL RAINFALL

Per Cent of Averages

Month	England and Wales	Scotland	Ireland	British Isles
January	71	49	57	63
February	49	54	129	67
March	13	24	24	18
April	57	76	51	61
May	103	107	109	105
June	78	124	83	91
July	79	108	119	96
August	79	139	119	104
September	37	73	38	47
October	120	144	127	128
November	232	130	151	188
December	190	168	184	183

Standard Sizes of Paper and Envelopes

International Paper Sizes

A3	297 × 420 mm	$11\frac{3}{4}$ × $16\frac{1}{2}$ in	
A4	297 × 210 mm	$8\frac{1}{4}$ × $11\frac{3}{4}$ in	
A5	210 × 148 mm	$8\frac{1}{4}$ × $5\frac{7}{8}$ in	

Standard envelopes for A4 paper measure
110 × 220 mm 8·7 × 4·3 in

English Paper Sizes

Octavo (8vo)	127 × 203 mm	5 × 8 in
Memorandum (memo.)	203 × 127 mm	8 × 5 in
Sixmo (6mo)	165 × 203 mm	$6\frac{1}{2}$ × 8 in
Quarto (4to)	203 × 254 mm	8 × 10 in
Foolscap (fcp.)	203 × 330 mm	8 × 13 in
Draft	254 × 406 mm	10 × 16 in
Brief	330 × 406 mm	13 × 16 in
Envelopes:—	152 × 89 mm	6 × $3\frac{1}{2}$ in
	229 × 120 mm	9 × 4 in

Addressing Envelopes

The address on an envelope must always be typed so that it runs parallel to the long side of the envelope—this is a Post Office regulation. At least $1\frac{1}{2}$ in. should be left at the top of the envelope above the address—this is also a Post Office regulation, and is designed to prevent the address from being obliterated by the Post Office date stamp. Any special instructions, such as "Personal" or "Confidential" should be typed two line spaces above the name of the addressee. This is particularly requested by the Post Office to ensure that nothing appears below the postcode.

Two methods are used for the typing of addresses on envelopes: the indented method (each line beginning half an inch to the right of the preceding line) and the block method (each line beginning at the same point on the scale): the latter is the more commonly used style. To ensure that the address is well displayed, it should be started half way down the envelope and approximately centred, horizontally.

The name of the post town should be typed in capital letters. A postcode should always be the last item of information in an address and it should not be punctuated: at least one space should be left between the two parts and it should never be underlined.

Window envelopes are widely used and save typing the name and address on the envelope: it must be borne in mind, however, that this method is only efficient if a standard place for the address is marked on the letter paper.

Exercise 112 shows some of the methods of typing addresses on envelopes.

Exercise 112

Type these addresses on envelopes, or on paper cut into oblongs measuring
8·7 × 4·3 in (110 × 220 mm) or 6 × $3\frac{1}{2}$ in (152 × 89 mm).

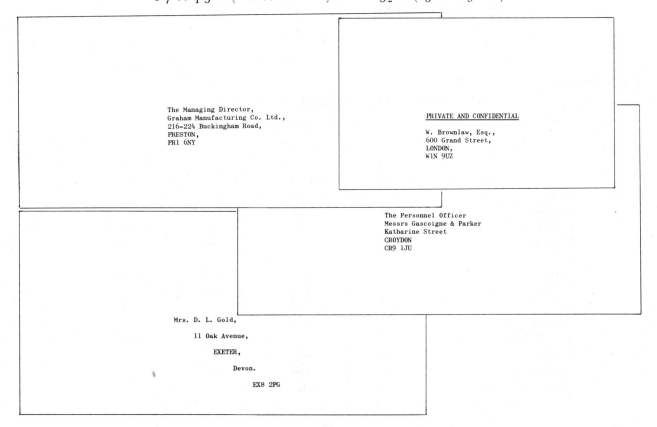

Exercise 117 (b)

POPULAR PETS

Budgerigars	Canaries	Goldfish	Guinea-pigs
Hamsters	Hedgehogs	Kittens	Newts
Parrots	Puppies	Rabbits	Snakes

Exercise 118

100 WORDS COMMONLY MISSPELT

absence	compulsorily	honorary	permissible
accessible	concession	humorous	possess
accommodate	concurrence	hygienic	preceding
achieved	conscientious	illegible	privilege
acknowledge	criticism	independent	pronunciation
acquainted	deficiency	indispensable	quarrelling
aerial	definite	insistent	queue
aggravate	disappoint	irresistible	received
allotted	disastrous	knowledge	referred
all right	discipline	maintenance	repetition
amateur	distinctive	marriage	rhythm
anxiety	eighth	Mediterranean	seize
appalling	eligible	miscellaneous	separate
argument	embarrassment	mischievous	simultaneous
automation	exaggerate	monotonous	sovereign
bachelor	exercise	mortgage	superfluous
bankruptcy	existence	necessary	supersede
beginning	February	negligible	suppress
benefited	foreign	occasionally	symmetry
brochure	forty	occurred	temporarily
catalogue	gauge	occurrence	twelfth
category	grievance	omitted	undoubtedly
committee	handkerchief	originally	until
commodity	harass	parallel	valuable
competent	height	permanent	woollen

Exercise 119

VISITORS TO STATELY HOMES

	1975	1976
Beaulieu, Hants (Lord Montague)	560,000	530,000
Longleat, Wilts (Marquess of Bath)	300,652	273,440
Blenheim, Oxon (Duke of Marlborough)	168,853	200,000
Harewood, Yorks (Earl of Harewood)	107,000	130,000
Hatfield, Herts (Marquess of Salisbury)	96,072	98,518
Blair Castle, Perthshire (Duke of Atholl)	86,548	92,230
Berkeley Castle, Glos (Mr. John Berkeley)	84,457	92,000
Castle Howard, Yorks (Mr. George Howard)	100,000	91,000
Inveraray Castle, Argyll (Duke of Argyll)	71,951	90,033

Exercise 113

Type the following addresses on envelopes, or on sheets of paper cut or folded to represent envelopes.
Type each address twice—in the punctuated and "open" style.
The post town should be typed in capitals.

1. Messrs. John Walker & Company, 21 Bryanston Street, London W1A 2AZ
2. David Hughes, Esq., B.A., The School House, Monport Street, Croydon CRO 3XY
3. Miss M. H. Berry, Oak Cottage, Stamford, Lincs. PE9 2YD
4. Master Michael Mackintosh, The Cedars School, Daventry, Northants. NN4 9ET
5. Personal, John Davidson, Esq., James Hadlow & Company Ltd., 16 Newport Street, London W1N 9UZ
6. Confidential, The Manager, The Roverbury Bank Ltd., 15 High Street, Bristol BS6 7AH
7. The Misses A. and D. Ellisson, 84 Church Street, Bath BA2 2BH
8. The Rev. Father Andrewes, The Presbytery, Sutton-in-Ashfield, Notts. NG17 5FT
9. George Ericson, Esq., M.C., M.A., F.R.Econ.Soc., 56 High Street, Sheffield S30 5AP
10. Sir George Andover, Bart., The Hall, Purley, Surrey CR2 4TJ
11. The Secretary, Davidson, Scott & Company Ltd., Imperial Buildings, Corquandale Street, Birmingham B24 9AH
12. The Rev. Michael O'Flynn, The Vicarage, Bourne, Lincs. PE10 9PB

As an additional exercise, type the names and addresses in alphabetical order.

Exercise 114

Type the following addresses on envelopes, or on sheets of
paper cut or folded to represent envelopes.
The post towns should be typed in capitals. The last four addresses
(9–12) should be typed without punctuation.

1. Major R. Mainwaring, R.A., Alderley Barracks, Towcester, Northants. NN12 7BY
2. Leading Seaman J. Smith P/JXA2345, Mess No. 6, H.M.S. Vernon, Portsmouth PO1 3ER
3. Mr. P. Murphy, 3 Main Street, Ballinamore Bridge, Ballinasloe, Co. Galway, Irish Republic.
4. Sir David Burkborough, C.B., Henby Hall, Leeds LS1 5BQ
5. Mrs. John Golding, 57 Church Street, Pinner, Middx. HA5 4PA
6. Mr. and Mrs. James Hadley and Family, The Larches, Abingley Road, Reading RG1 3BU
7. Mr. A. Williams, 514 Kingsbridge Road, Derby DE1 8ZL
8. The Occupier, 58 Rendon Road, Nottingham NG11 9DY
9. The Lady Peter Deauville, Old Bond Street, London W1X 4AN
10. Alexander Beauchamp, Esq., 82 Grove Court Mansions, New Road, Brighton BN1 1UF
11. The Headmaster, Bolton School, Rougier Street, York YO1 1HR
12. Mrs. Mary Sydenham, 11 Clarendon Road, Watford WD1 1HS

As an additional exercise, type the names and addresses in alphabetical order.

TABULATION AND DISPLAY

Before starting to type tabular work, clear all previous margin and tabular stops. Count the number of characters in the widest line in each column and add together the totals. Subtract this number from the number of characters that you can type across a sheet of paper (pica type gives ten characters, elite gives twelve characters to the inch). This leaves the number of spaces to be divided between the spaces between the columns and the left- and right-hand margins. Set tabular stops for each column where most items begin; slight deviations from the stops can be made by means of the space bar or back-spacer.

In such documents as balance sheets, it is essential that the debit and credit sides should be evenly balanced. If a long carriage machine is not available two sheets of paper may be used and joined together afterwards. Always type the side containing the larger number of items first, marking in pencil on the second sheet the points at which you must start and finish typing.

To centre a piece of work vertically on the page, count the number of lines the piece of work will occupy, deduct this number from the number of lines that can be typed on the size of paper you are using (six lines of single-space typing occupy 1 in (25 mm) of paper with both pica and elite type) and then divide the space available between the top and bottom margins.

Use the underscore for ruling totals. Type the first line immediately under the final item; then turn up two single-line spaces and type the total figures. Turn up one single-line space before typing the final line. Turn the paper up again slightly, using the interliner, and complete the double ruling. The £ should be typed in front of the total figure. Study the example in Exercise 134.

Tabular statements are more effective and clearer when ruled and one of the following methods should be followed:—

1. *Typed rules*—Type the horizontal lines by means of the underscore, extending them two spaces into the margins at either side, then mark lightly either by pencil or a stencil dot the points for the vertical lines. Remove the paper and reinsert sideways and then type the vertical lines by means of the underscore—care being taken not to extend these lines beyond the horizontal lines.

2. *Lines made by ball-pen or pencil*—Most modern typewriters have two small notches or round holes on the alignment scale. Insert the point of a pencil or fine ball-pen in one of these notches/holes and hold against the paper with the right hand. Move the carriage from one side to the other by means of the carriage release lever and you will obtain a continuous horizontal line. To make a vertical line, release the platen ratchet by means of the interliner (see page 52) and turn the platen up with the left-hand knob.

3. *Inked lines*—If the lines are to be ruled in ink, remove paper when table is completed and with a fine nib (preferably a draughtsman's pen) rule lines carefully and neatly to the marked points which can be made by means of stencil dots or lightly marked with a pencil. Always wipe the edge of the ruler after ruling each line to prevent smudging. (A ball-point pen can also be used with this method.)

Exercise 117 (a)

FROZEN VEGETABLES

Asparagus	Carrots	Onions
Peas	Celery	Spinach
Brocoli	Corn	Sprouts

SPECIAL SIGNS AND COMBINATION CHARACTERS

The following exercise gives practice in the typing of special signs and combination characters, i.e. symbols which are not included on the typewriter keyboard. In order to produce these characters it may be necessary to type one character, backspace and then type the second character, or alternatively hold down the space bar and strike the two keys in succession. If it is necessary to raise or lower the platen before typing the second character, as in the degree sign, the INTER-LINER, a lever usually on the left side of the carriage, which frees the platen from the ratchet control, can be used. When the lever is returned to its normal position the typewriter will automatically return to the original line of writing. Alternatively if your typewriter is fitted with half-line spacing mechanism, it is easier to raise or lower the line of typing one-half space by turning the platen knob.

The majority of typists use these special characters only occasionally. Should the work of the typist call for the frequent use of them, it is possible for an exchange of keys to be made, and for the required character to be substituted for one that is not often used.

The asterisk and the daggers are used to refer to footnotes. They and the degree sign, which are typed above the line of type, are called "superior" characters. Characters which appear below the line of type are called "inferior" characters—e.g. H_2SO_4.

Exercise 115

Margin stops: Pica 11; Elite 19
Tab. stops: 31 and 45; 39 and 54 (26 spaces allowed for third column)

Line-space lever for double-line spacing.

Asterisk	*	Small x and hyphen
Cedilla	ç	Comma under the c
Cent	C or c	Capital or small c
Dagger	†	Capital I and hyphen
Dash	as –	One hyphen with a space before and after
Decimal point	12.7	Full stop
Degree	59°	Small o
Diaeresis	ü	Quotation marks
Division	÷	Colon and hyphen
Double Dagger	‡	Two capital I's using interliner or capital I and equals sign
Dollar	$	Capital S and /
Equation	=	Two hyphens one typed slightly above the other using interliner
Exclamation mark	!	Apostrophe and full stop
Feet or Minutes	4'	Apostrophe
Fractions	5 1/5 or $5\frac{1}{5}$	Any fraction may be made up in either of these forms using interliner
Inches or Seconds	3"	Quotation marks
Minus	2 – 1	Hyphen
Multiplication	2 x 2	Small x
Per cent	%	Two small o's and / using interliner
Section	§ or §	Two large or small s's using interliner

Roman Numerals

Roman numerals are used for a number of purposes, some of which are mentioned in Exercise 116.

I is used for	. .	1
V is used for	. .	5
X is used for	. .	10
L is used for	. .	50
C is used for	. .	100
D is used for	. .	500
M is used for	. .	1,000

When a character is followed by one of equal or less value, the whole expression denotes the sum of the values of the single characters, as:– VI = 6; XV = 15; LI = 51; CV = 105.

When a character is preceded by one of less value, the whole expression denotes the difference of the values of the single characters, as:– IV = 4; XL = 40.

A line drawn over any roman numeral multiplies it by one thousand, as:– $\overline{VI}$ = 6,000; $\overline{M}$ = 1,000,000

Roman numerals can be typed in capital or small characters. When capitals are used, the figure one is represented by the Capital **I**.

Exercise 116

Large roman numerals are mainly used for chapter headings (I), paragraphs (II), contents lists (III), in plays, to number Acts (IV), for monarchs (King George V), class and form numbers (Form Upper VI), examination stages (R.S.A. Stage III) and over buildings to show age (MDCCCLXXX).

Small roman numerals (i, ii, iii, iv, v, vi, vii, viii, ix, x) are used mainly for inset paragraphs in rules, regulations and reports, clauses within sections, numbering the pages of prefaces, verse references in books and plays, and bible references.

When typing roman numerals, care must be taken to ensure (a) that the unit figures are in line with each other and (b) that the numerals are arranged so that at least half an inch is left between the margin or paragraph indentation and the longest group of numerals – as in the following example:–

Hours of work shall be guaranteed as follows:–

    (i)   the guaranteed work shall be 40 hours;

    (ii) the guaranteed day or night to be worked on Monday to Friday inclusive shall be 8 hours;

   (iii) the guaranteed day or night on a Saturday, Sunday or declared holiday shall be 8 hours.